A leader with an amazing dream influencing a multitude of individuals with a relaxed strength and an ability to develop friendship across cultures are only a couple of reasons why this book arrests my attention. This book uniquely portrays Ken Johnson as a man with a deep passion for life, a person to serve others, a passion for missions, a strong work ethic, and, most importantly, the desire to know God deeply and intimately. Highly regarded by both peers and friends, alike, indeed, Dr. Ken Johnson is "A MAN WORTH KNOWING."

Kenneth L. Mills
District Superintendent
Mid-Atlantic District Church of the Nazarene
Shippensburg, PA

This book is a great tribute to Ken! It certainly captures the breadth and depth of his capabilities, intellect, and character. His exceptional people skills enabled him to relate and function with everyone he encountered in his brief time on earth. The information in this story confirmed to me all of the positive and enthusiastic comments I have heard about Ken and the impact he had during his time at ONU! His legacy will live on in the success on the School of Engineering and its graduates! Thank you for giving me the opportunity for reading this life story of a very remarkable Christian leader.

"Skip" Walker
Martin D. Walker School of Engineering (ONU)
Carmel, IN

TREMENDOUS! I have never met Dr. Ken Johnson but after reading, An Unexpected Finish Line Leaves A Unique Legacy, I have now met Dr. Ken Johnson! What vivid memories, stories, and tributes have been collected about an outstanding educator, missioneer, athlete, husband, father, son, and friend of thousands. Ken Johnson died at age 43. Our son Dave, at age 45. My heart knows how the entire Johnson family feels—there aren't enough words to explain it. All I can say is—what a powerful and godly legacy left by this outstanding child of God, Dr. Ken Johnson.

Dr. James H. Diehl
General Superintendent Emeritus
Church of the Nazarene
Denver, CO

Billions around the globe claim a faith in Jesus Christ. Far fewer lead lives that exhibit the "new creation" that the Bible describes. Unfortunately, significantly fewer still show a Sprit-led lifestyle that is an evidence of that leadership. Dr. Ken Johnson was one of the latter. Multiple individuals have testified to the difference that their association with Ken made in their lives. His sermon in 2012 on stewardship was outstanding, yet the sermon of his life has had a far greater impact on the world.

He was a man worth knowing… would that I had had the blessing of that association. I strongly recommend this book for "searchers" of all ages.

R. W. Mann, M.D.
Cook Children's Medical Center
Fort Worth, TX

Table of Contents

FriesenPress

Suite 300 - 990 Fort St
Victoria, BC, V8V 3K2
Canada

www.friesenpress.com

Copyright © 2016 by David Johnson and Jerri Johnson
First Edition — 2016

ISBN
978-1-4602-8307-3 (Hardcover)
978-1-4602-8308-0 (Paperback)
978-1-4602-8309-7 (eBook)

1. BIOGRAPHY & AUTOBIOGRAPHY, RELIGIOUS

Distributed to the trade by The Ingram Book Company

Acknowledgements

We would like to take this opportunity to thank all the people who have contributed to this book. It was such a sudden and shocking loss, and the outpouring we saw stands as the greatest tribute to our late son. This book came together so those who knew Ken, even if only for a spell, can have a fuller picture of the impact he left.

To our friends and family, thank you for sharing your stories of Ken. We know many of them were deep and intimate personal memories and not easily articulated so soon after his passing.

To Ken's co-workers, we knew so little about our son's professional life, certainly not the abundance we learned from the things you told us. He was a man of great achievement but often too humble to broadcast that success. We thank you for providing vignettes of a dedicated, hard-working servant.

To Ken's students, we are sorry you only had our son among you for such a short amount of time. We know from your stories how profoundly he affected you in that time, and he shared with us often how you were changing his life. May you continue to seek knowledge of the world and of God the Father.

We would like to especially thank Dr. John C. Bowling, the President of Olivet Nazarene University (ONU) where our son was working at the time of his passing. Dr. Bowling's compassionate leadership in the immediate aftermath of unexpected loss was felt not only among the students, staff, and faculty of ONU but also among the members of Ken's family. Such grace and understanding should not go unacknowledged.

Special gratitude is also extended to Mr. David Tait, Col. William Black, Mrs. Jennifer Johnson, Ms. Marie Johnson, Mr. Jeff Jorge, and Mr. Timothy Quinn for financially making this epistolary biography possible. They believed strongly enough in the life story of Ken to help our family fund this project, and we are eternally thankful for their vision and support.

Our project editors, Mr. James Phillips, Dr. Thalyta Swanepoel, and Marjorie Vinson devoted countless hours to curating a thread from dozens of personal stories, and trimming that thread into a single cohesive narrative about Ken's life. They deserve special recognition.

Lastly, to Ken's family: Jen for loving our son and being a fantastic mother to our grandchildren, Sydney, for the timeless hours she spent helping us on the computer, Erick and Luke for continued support, and Bethany, for the beautiful picture she drew for the book. The strength you have shown over the nearly last three years has meant everything to us as parents. We certainly could not have gone through this without your beautiful family alongside us. We love you to the moon and back a million times over.

Editors' Note

This story is a biography about Ken Johnson, but it's not your traditional biography. When considering how to best tell the story of Ken's impact on the people whom he met, the answer was immediately apparent: have others tell the story for us. Because of the epistolary, or letter-based, nature of the story, we, the editors, had the task of shaping those letters into a fully fleshed-out story.

When letters were first collected, we didn't know the nature or the scope of the project. As our plans and focus began to coalesce around the vision here executed, it meant some letters became either superfluous or non-advancing in respect to the narrative. It meant that some contributions, while perfectly poignant, fell by the wayside. We don't mean to say those specific recollections of Dr. Johnson were any less than the others; they simply didn't fit in this particular telling of his story.

We edited letters for voice, so even if we had fifty different story tellers the over-arching thread would read with a consistent tone and timbre. There was no need to edit for content because each memory of Ken already had a vivid life that needed no embellishment and no addition. This project was a labor of love, one in which we endeavored always to tell the best story we could about a man worth knowing, Dr. Ken Johnson. We hope you enjoy reading about his life as much as we did.

Dr. Thalyta Swanepoel
Mr. James Phillips
Mrs. Marjorie Vinson

Foreword

A legacy is heritage, something passed down from previous generations. A legacy is what lives on after you die: your imprint. The question is not whether you *will* leave a legacy, but what *kind* of legacy you will leave. Will it involve attributes like humility, faithfulness, service, and love? Many of us are familiar with the legacies of such noteworthy people as Dr. Martin Luther King, Jr. and Mother Theresa, but what about legacies of people who are not well-known: people like us and perhaps people like you? What about the legacies left by those living ordinary lives, making small continual impacts day to day with the choices they make and the paths they choose? Whether or not we realize it, we are all forging a legacy to be left after we are no longer here to shape it.

To help you reflect on the legacy you are creating, we invite you to read the incredible story of our son, Dr. Kenneth Edwin Johnson. He died suddenly at the age of 43, about two miles from the finish line of the annual Iceman Cometh Challenge, a 30-mile mountain bike race from Kalkaska to Traverse City, MI, on November 2, 2013.

In the time following his death, we heard things about Ken we never knew. A humble man, our son did not talk about his accomplishments. Together with Dave Tait, who collaborated with Ken for 20 years, we decided to document Ken's life in the hope his story might inspire others.

To aid in this endeavor, we solicited contributions from many people who had significant relationships with him during the different times of his life: people who knew him as a brother, husband, father, uncle, nephew, cousin, friend, pastor, colleague, teacher, and student. The stories and letters we received were compiled into a book, the very book you hold in your hands. Together, they weave in and out of various times in Ken's life. They tell how he affected those around him from the time he first opened his eyes until now, well after he passed away.

As a child, Ken was hyper, energetic, creative, and intensely competitive, not knowing for a long time how to lose with grace. He was a challenging little boy, stealing and lying at a young age, but he was also a joy to raise. He was an avid reader; he loved doing magic tricks, and playing Monopoly and chess. He enjoyed sports, loved making paper airplanes, and was a big fan of *Star Wars*.

During his teen years, he developed into a handsome young man with many gifts, talents, and interests. He became a high achiever and earned many honors, including two patents.

He entered Eastern Michigan University (EMU) on an art scholarship, joined the Marine Reserves, and became a Squad Leader. Later, he transferred schools and finished his degree in engineering at ONU, in Illinois, where he met and fell in love with his wife, Jen, and later returned to teach.

Our son's career—holding multiple jobs and owning a couple of companies along the way—was marked by challenge and triumph, but through hard work and perseverance, Ken became a highly successful engineer. In spite of that success, he never neglected his true passion: missions work. During their marriage, Ken, Jen, and their four children were always deeply involved in the life of their church, where Ken made multiple trips overseas, serving the church in various capacities.

We pray, as you join us for the journey through our son's life, that you will think about the impact you are making right now, about what you want your legacy to be, and how you can daily serve as an example of Christ's love to those around you.

While we miss our son greatly, we understand and truly believe that everything has a reason and that God's purposes are greater than ours. We consider it an honor and a privilege to serve as your guides as we hear together how the 43 years our son spent on earth impacted the people he knew, starting with the first people who knew him: us.

1
Stepping Back in Time

Dave Johnson
FATHER

As products of both nature and nurture, children have their parents to thank for a large portion of who they become during their formative years. Truthfully, they have their parents to thank, and their parents' parents, back through their family trees, because each successive generation has an impact on how the future develops. This idea of values, systems, and traits passed over time is referred to by sociologists and cultural anthropologists as "generational transference."

While some squander the opportunity to develop holistically the positives they want to see in their children, both Jerri and I were raised in such a way as to value heavily the unique relationships parents have with their children, and we sought to give to our family the same values and characteristics instilled in us by our own parents. We wanted any generational transference that came from us to be as positive as it could be.

As an avid reader, I came across a book by Jimmy Evans on this idea of positive generational transference. In the book, the author lays out what he thinks are important pillars of doing transference right. We must have a system of values, not just things that are important to us, mind you, but an interconnected system, an ethos that characterizes our entire way of thinking. We must understand we are not just passing on to our children those systems, but we need an awareness that we are seeking to establish multigenerational impact with our decisions. Finally, transference requires a selflessness by which we see ourselves as owners and possessors of nothing, merely stewards entrusted to guard, protect, and uphold that with which we have been charged. If such a point of view can be established—a point of view, I might add, countercultural in possibly the most self-centered, self-seeking time in history—then it makes the other two come as logical progressions.

Jerri and I didn't have these ideas fleshed out in a lovely book when we decided to start a family, but we did have an inherent understanding of those principles. This is why we believe it is important that you understand our childhoods, Jerri's and mine, in brevity, because in them you see the values taught to us that we sought to teach our children. And Ken, for better or for worse, is as much a product of our collective youths as he was his own.

* * *

I, Dave, am an only child. I was born on November 8, 1939, to Carl Edwin and Helen Sestina Johnson. Unfortunately, my mother died when I was three years old. I really don't remember her except for the few things people told me about her: She wanted me to be a missionary to Africa, she was a strong Christian, her parents came from Hungary, she was one of seven children, a peace maker, and played the violin.

My father was also a wonderful Christian. His parents came from Sweden and their names are printed on Ellis Island in New York. My parents were members of the Salvation Army Church in Ridgway, PA, where I grew up.

For the next half decade, my father was a single parent. During those intervening years, a number of my aunts and uncles on both sides of my family helped my dad take care of me. My maternal grandmother spent a lot of time at our apartment cooking and doing housework for us (she cooked for Royalty in Hungary before she came to the U.S.). She was a member of the Lutheran Church and a great Christian influence in my life.

When my dad married Elsie McDonald, I was eight years old. They went to Niagara Falls, NY, for their honeymoon, and I asked them to bring me back a real helicopter. I knew it was a silly request, but I still asked for it. After they returned, Elsie and my father became members of the newly formed Church of the Nazarene in Ridgway.

Dad was a mail carrier for the U.S. Postal Service and later became a salesman. I remember sitting beside him in church, singing with him, and often laying my head on his lap at some point during the sermon.

In my youth, I was involved in typical childhood activities. I was a Boy Scout, joined the YMCA where I learned to swim, played Little League baseball, and had a paper route. In junior high and high school, I participated in many sports, musical groups, served on the yearbook staff, and was Vice President of my Senior class. Betty Hoffman, who played the piano at our church, nurtured my musical interests. I also spent many hours at my Uncle Art's and Aunt Mary's house. Uncle Art was my dad's brother. Their six children, in many ways, became my siblings.

For a year after high school, I worked at a research laboratory at Keystone Carbon Co. in St. Mary's, PA. At the end of 1958, I enrolled at Eastern Nazarene College (ENC), in Quincy, MA to study mathematics and general science. I paid for my education using money I had saved, my $100 activities scholarship, $100 from my parents, money I made singing in the college quartets and doing other jobs, and student loans. My parents said this was all they could give me each year. I continued to participate in sports and music during my college years. I was a member of several male quartets that traveled on the weekends during the school year and in the summer, representing the college. Midway through my college experience, my dad died suddenly of a heart attack.

In the fall of my senior year at ENC, I spotted a beautiful freshman with a bubbly, cheerful personality. Her name was Jerri Jones. I knew and really liked her older brother, Bill, and her sister, Ruth Ann, who also studied at ENC. Jerri and I got along well, and we were married at the end of the following summer.

Jerri Johnson
MOTHER

I was born the third child of a Nazarene pastor, the Reverend Jerold Kenneth Jones, and Mary Emma Morgan Jones at the Episcopal Hospital in Philadelphia, PA. I have one older brother and one older sister. Being lucky to have a great Christian heritage, I was in church every time the doors were open. Many a night, when I would go to bed, I would hear my dad in his bedroom praying for my siblings and me, all individually. My parents were honest and faithful, and they practiced what they preached. I am eternally grateful for their example.

My mother entertained all the time. Every Sunday she would set the table for ten people. There were only five in our family, but she was always prepared for visitors or military men. We also housed all of the traveling evangelists who came to our church. As children, we enjoyed having company in our home. My father being a practical joker, we were encouraged to play pranks on our visitors, which made those times even more fun. Our family spent every summer in Cape May, NJ, where my dad was president of Erma Holiness Campground, and my mom did more entertaining.

I lived a normal life. I played in mud puddles, was a cheerleader in middle school, went on dates, enjoyed football and basketball games, and attended district rallies with the church. In high school, I was president of the Future Nurses Club. Like many teenagers, I was perfectly content playing the part of a good Christian. Because I grew up in the church, I knew how to act and what to say. Near the end of high school, however, God became much more personal to me, and I developed a relationship with Him beyond the religion I'd inherited from my parents.

After graduating from high school, I attended ENC. While I dated often, it wasn't until I started seeing a certain senior that I knew what I was looking for. His name was David Carl Johnson, and I enjoyed his company very much. He was funny, athletic, popular, and sang low bass in a few quartets. In March 1963, we became engaged at the Title Basin in Washington, DC, and we married on August 24, 1963. My mother made everything for our reception and my father performed the ceremony.

Our family eventually consisted of Dave and me, plus our four children: Sonya, Whitnie, Ken, and Erica. They became the most important aspect of what we were doing. They were the cornerstone around which Dave and I were building our future.

Deeply respecting how our families raised us, Dave and I vowed to raise our children similarly. I got pregnant three months after our wedding. Our oldest daughter Sonya Renee, was born on August 15, 1964, in Washington, DC. We were both so happy to become parents. When Sonya was about nineteen months old, I got pregnant again. This pregnancy was high risk, and six months into my term, I lost a set of twin boys.

During the week I spent in the hospital, Dave was keeping a commitment to lead the music for a revival at a local church. He could not be at the hospital in the evenings or during the day, but he would pop in between teaching at Crosslands High School and his evening revival job. He would bring me papers and tests to grade for his students.

The doctor told me I should not get pregnant for at least one year, but six months later, I was going to have another baby. Daughter number two, Whitnie Elaine, was born on May 18, 1967, in Athens, GA, where Dave was working on his master's degree. She had big brown eyes and smiled all of the time.

A little over two years later, guess what, another baby. Finally, a boy. Kenneth Edwin was born on July 8, 1970. Dave had just finished his doctorate in mathematics education at the University of Georgia (UGA), in Athens, GA. We were all so happy to have a boy since we lost the twins. I remember noticing that Ken did not cry much, even on the drive to Marquette, MI, shortly after his birth. We were moving our family there for a teaching position Dave had accepted in the mathematics department at Northern Michigan University (NMU).

Three and a half years later, baby number four was on the way. Another daughter, Erica Dawn, was born on April 30, 1974, in Ann Arbor, MI. Erica was a sweetheart but had a mind of her own.

Although we, of course, were not perfect parents, we laughed a lot, had family devotions, and prayed together often. We took active roles in church, school, and community and encouraged Ken to be involved as well. Many college students and foreign exchange students lived with us for periods of time, which enriched all our lives. Another high priority we made was to get together with aunts, uncles, cousins, etc. as often as possible for Thanksgiving, water-skiing, picnicking, berry-picking, and other events. These interactions allowed Ken and his cousin, Ryan Miller, to become best friends and for Ken to look forward periodically for our family to return to Pennsylvania for fun and fellowship with the Johnson clan.

A friend recently stated that the way Ken developed can be directly related to the way we raised him. While we could take credit for the feat, we are eternally grateful for all who played a role in nurturing him, because who he became certainly didn't happen entirely of our own accord.

2
The Early Years

"Train a child in the way he should go, and when
he is old, he will not turn from it."

Proverbs 22:6 (NIV)

Jerri
MOTHER

When Ken was born and I wrote his name, "Kenneth Edwin Johnson," I thought how nice it looked together. Kenneth was the middle name of his grandfather on my side, and Edwin was the middle name of his grandfather on Dave's side. When Ken was about three weeks old his godparents, Joy and Glenn Rose, came from Maryland to visit us in Georgia. We were preparing to move to Marquette, MI.

Ken 3 weeks old with his God-Mother Joy Rose

Joy and I packed a U-Haul trailer and started driving to Marquette with three children, including three-week-old baby Ken. We'd travelled only 250 yards when the trailer started swaying ominously. We immediately turned around and drove home to have our husbands repack its contents. Joy and I traveled to Grand Rapids, MI, where we spent the night with family. The next morning, shortly after setting out for Marquette, we had a flat tire right in front of the police station. I cannot remember whether the police fixed it or if they called someone to do it. In any case, Ken's two sisters screamed when the police came outside because they thought they were going to be put in jail.

We arrived in Marquette about 10 p.m., but there were no vacancies within 30 miles. We spent the night at the home of Bill Mutch, a fellow graduate student at the UGA, and new coworker in the mathematics department at NMU.

The following day I went house--hunting and bought a home after having consulted with local friends and with Dave over the telephone.

And so the first big trip of Ken's life, though he was blissfully unaware at the time, was over.

During this time, when Ken was 6 months old, his feet were turning in and we got a brace to straighten them. He learned to crawl with the brace connecting his two feet.

Politely, Ken was a rambunctious child. During the three years we lived in Marquette, Ken scared me half to death more than once. For example, when he was supposed to be taking a nap, I received a phone call telling me Ken was downtown at the local department store six blocks away. I still don't know how he got out. Another time a man knocked on the front door in the middle of the night. He was white as a ghost and holding Ken. The man had found Ken in the middle of Front Street, a one-way, two-lane road that ran in front of our house. In the interest of his safety and our peace of mind, we decided to put a lock on Ken's door.

One Sunday morning I had just finished getting Sonya and Whitnie ready for church. I walked downstairs to find Ken, dressed in a white one-piece suit, sitting in the middle of the wood burning fireplace. The suit, covered in soot, had to be thrown away. Ken was put in the bathtub where I tried to get the soot off of him. Needless to say, we made it to church late. Ken had black marks all over him from where the soot would not come off with soap and water.

When he was two and one half years old, Ken slid down the basement steps on his stomach, pulled a chair over to the furnace, and stuck his head inside. He was getting ready to climb in the hole when I found him. I pulled him out and got him upstairs just before it cycled on. Then there was the time I found him on the balcony of his bedroom, eating pigeon droppings. We called the humane society to come and get the pigeons. We put a lock on the balcony door, too, just for good measure.

As if that wasn't enough, the pastor's wife called me and said she wanted to talk with me about my lack of control over Ken. "If she only knew," I thought. I enjoy the humor of these stories now, but at the time, they only served to exhaust and terrify me.

When it came time for potty-training, I was downright anxious. We got Ken potty-trained at night, so he would be dry in the mornings, but it was difficult during the day. We bought him a little plastic bubblegum machine, and every time he used the toilet, he put a penny in and got a piece of bubble gum. One day, he fell down the steps holding his bubble gum machine and it broke. He had gotten so used to that reward system that he struggled for a while, and it took another couple of months to get him totally trained without it.

When Ken was two and one half, he got pneumonia and had to be admitted to the hospital, completely quarantined. Only Dave and I could be in his room, one at a time. I was with him most of the time since Dave had to work. It was very difficult as a parent to put on a mask when I went in, knowing I could do nothing to help my child. Ken wanted to leave the room and move around and run and play, but he couldn't.

Ken age 3

After 3 years in Marquette, we moved to Ann Arbor because Dave had accepted an assistant professor position in the mathematics department at EMU. During the winter that year, Ken and his sisters enjoyed many toboggan rides with Dave steering down the hills at Getty's Lake.

Nine months after moving to Ann Arbor, Ken's younger sister, Erica, was born. I remember how badly Ken wanted a little brother. When we had Erica, he kept saying, "My brother is so cute," and he would often make comments about what a good boy she was. It took a while, but we eventually got him to concede that his sister was indeed a girl.

During the time we lived in Ann Arbor, Ken learned how to ride a bike. The little boy across the street already knew how to ride a bike, and he was younger than Ken, a fact that motivated Ken to master the bicycle as soon as possible. Dave remembers the day he let go of the bike seat and left Ken to ride on his own.

After meeting the pastor of the Ypsilanti Free Methodist Church at a garage sale, we began attending services there and continued doing so for 20 years. Carole Richardson, Ken's kindergarten Sunday school teacher, was one of many people in his youth to comment on Ken's exuberance. His hyperactivity was often kindly worded when described to us. "He has lots of energy," they would say.

In 1976, after having attended that church for a number of months, we decided to buy a wooded 2.5-acre property with a stream flowing through it. We began building a house on the property and would raise our family there once it was completed. Ken later said that it was a great place for a little boy to grow up. Indeed, Ken and his friends really enjoyed playing there. Ken passed through his youth and into adolescence, and, much like other young children, it was a tumultuous time of learning from mistakes and growing out of bad habits.

On the way home from church one Sunday, the girls told us Ken had been giving money to a bunch of kids, so we told him to meet us in his bedroom when we got home. We asked him where he got the money. "From the big sand hill," next to where we live, he said. After much questioning and talking to his sisters, we discovered Ken was not telling the truth. He had taken it from a little bank in the children's section of our church. We had a conversation with Ken about stealing, then and there. Six years old is plenty old enough to know that stealing is wrong, and lying all the same. We prayed with him and said he'd owe the pastor an apology when he gave back the money the next time we were at church.

After the evening service that night, I told Ken to go see the pastor. To our dismay, Ken did not apologize; he simply gave back the money and ran away. We found out later, to add to the problem, Ken had not returned all the money. Indeed, he kept back enough to continue doling it out to other children at church.

Another time Ken stole some candy from a gift shop on Nixon Road in Ann Arbor. I called the woman working at the store and told her he would be returning the candy. Before the candy was returned, I prayed with him asking God again to forgive him for stealing. This was certainly not something for which I wanted my son to be known. Then he prayed, asking God to help him stop stealing. I drove him to the store and waited outside. When he returned, he still had the stolen chocolate coin wrapped in gold foil. So much for his prayer, I thought. I marched him right back in the store and called for the manager. When she came, I went back outside so she could speak privately with Ken about his choices. She told him how bad it was for him to take something not belonging to him, then she praised him for returning the chocolate.

By the time Ken was ready to start school full time, Dave and I were relieved. We hoped that having more structure to each day with additional authority figures in his life would help Ken find more constructive ways to channel his vast amounts of energy and enthusiasm. He was learning, just as many young boys do, that his actions have consequences. It was our hope he would begin to understand not all consequences have to be bad; good can come from the choices we make.

Erica Johnson
SISTER

Ken and I were the youngest two in our family, so we were home together the most while we were growing up. We played together nicely, but, like all siblings, could fight with or without provocation. We made castles out of blocks, gave toy cars their own parking spaces, and played all sorts of make believe. When we fought, we were sent to our rooms. The only ticket out of jail was to apologize and play nicely. Knowing the penance we had to pay, we would send paper airplanes to one another with notes of collaboration.

"Okay, let's apologize and tell Mom what she needs to hear so we can get out." We also shared details of the story we'd tell Mom so we could be consistent. It's a testament to the bond siblings share that being sent to our rooms for fighting resulted in the two of us working together to get out of trouble. After we got everything straightened between us, we'd call for our mom and make our pleas for pardon and carry on with our fun.

One of Ken's favorite things to do when we were little was to adopt characters to play. Even into high school, he loved pretending to be a hot-shot model, of whom I was expected to take pictures, and over whom his visiting friends were expected to fawn. Of course, I never minded playing along; my brother had some cute friends. Sometimes, it got embarrassing, just due to the nature of the fashions of our youth. Ken and his friends had some awfully short shorts that, when climbing trees or other objects, would expose that which best remained unseen. I remember feeling embarrassed quite often as a result of their wardrobe malfunctions, but such is the life for a popular model and his entourage.

We were also on the cutting edge of filmmaking as children. Ken, our cousins Ryan and Rebecca, and I would often put on our own productions, putting the full scale of our collective imaginations to use. Ken and Ryan shot flaming arrows at us, fed us bread and water as their slaves, locked us in cages as their pets, and even made our own version of *Rocky*. Ryan and Ken had marvelous ideas, and Rebecca and I naïvely played along. I'm sure some of those videos survived the years, and I would love to see our hilarity in youth.

Around the time we were in junior high, I remember Ken making traps for me in the woods. He would dig holes that were three to five feet deep and cover them with sticks and leaves. They were holes of the kind one might see on Looney Tunes and other children's shows. He would try to get me to chase him through the woods so I would fall into one of his pits. I'm sure he didn't think how badly I could have broken an arm or a leg wiping out into a hole five feet deep, but he tried nonetheless. Luckily, I was never seriously injured, but Ken put all of his ingenuity into making my maiming a reality.

When his friends spent the night, I would always be their waitress for meal times. I had menus with prices for the available food in the house. I took their orders, made their food, and served them. They even paid me, and sometimes I got tips.

Looking back, I think I was, as the youngest child, sometimes used as a living play-thing, even when I was nearly 16. At the time, I just enjoyed being included and partaking in the fun with my older brother. Even though we fought often, I typically remember the fun above all else. Ken had a powerful imagination. As a child, it got him and his accomplices a good scolding every now and again, but in his adulthood, I think it served him incredibly well.

There were times I wanted to hit him, and I'm sure I did, because my brother frustrated me as much as he made me smile, but that tension is part of growing up. He wasn't perfect, and I certainly wasn't either, but as his sister, I saw him at his best and his worst. I had the privilege of seeing him grow up ahead of me, of learning from the mistakes he made, and of having his wisdom available to me when I wanted it.

3
The Elementary School Years

Jerri
MOTHER

In April 1979, Dave went to Swaziland, a small country landlocked between South Africa and Mozambique, accompanied by Ken and Whitnie. Dave accepted a short-term appointment as the mathematics advisor for a USAID curriculum-writing project for grades 1-7, involving the education authorities and EMU. What initially was a two-month appointment, became a four-month adventure.

The first days in Swaziland were really eventful, being filled with all the things you'd think could occupy early time spent in a new country. Ken lost a jacket on the plane, which the airline could not track down. Dave and the kids tried new Swazi foods. Ken and Whitnie met other missionary children their age, like their life-long friend Kevin Wardlaw. It was a whirlwind, figuring how to adapt in a foreign place when it was so far removed from any experience they'd had.

While Whitnie spent some of those first days at a church campout at Piggs Peak, a town in northwestern Swaziland, Ken and Dave spent quality time playing Monopoly, Ken's favorite game by far. In the beginning, Dave would give Ken a break while they were playing, maybe not putting hotels on some critical properties. Ken, being the competitive imp he was, took advantage of his father's mercy. It wasn't long before Ken was thrashing Dave without help, at which point Dave lost interest in the game.

Dave and the children quickly learned how to shop at the market, go to the bank, enroll in school, and many other routine tasks associated with moving. They relaxed by visiting the Mlilwane Wildlife Sanctuary, described today as Swaziland's pioneer conservation area, in the Ezulwini Valley, and Kruger National Park in northeastern South Africa, one of the biggest game parks on the continent.

Ken at Sydney Williams school, Swaziland, Africa

I went to visit for a couple of weeks that June. We spent two days in Durban on the eastern seaboard of South Africa, and two days in Hluhluwe, a small town in northern KwaZulu-Natal. At the Game Reserve, Ken petted a giraffe whose name was Sweetie Pie. We took a river ride in the town of Saint Lucia where we saw hippos and crocodiles. Before we left, however, I noticed the gas gauge was near empty and pointed it out to the man steering the boat, a small rowboat with a motor. He had a little bit of fun with me and said in South Africa "E" meant "enough" and "F" meant "finished," before he went to get petrol.

The morning I was set to leave with the kids, Ken and Dave took a gold mine tour while Whitnie and I went shopping in downtown Johannesburg with members of a missionary family at the local Free Methodist Church with whom we usually stayed when we were in Johannesburg. Ken and Dave had the opportunity to witness how a gold bar about the size of a brick is made. When it had cooled, some people in the tour group, including Ken, had the chance to hold the bar. Dave recalls jokingly planning with Ken how to escape with the ingot stowed in their pockets.

Ken with his head in a crocodile's mouth Swaziland, Africa

That evening, Ken, Whitnie, and I boarded a KLM Airlines flight to Detroit, MI, with stops in Brussels and Boston. During the flight, Ken asked the flight attendant if he could go to the cockpit to see what it looked like. He was thrilled and a little disbelieving when they gave him permission.

Ken in the cockpit, KLM Airlines

Ken with flight attendants, KLM Airlines

When we arrived in Brussels, there was a problem at the check-in counter. When it finally got resolved, my family was seated in first class on our way home. I told the children to act as if they had purchased the tickets, and indeed had the right composure to sit in first class. I knew in all likelihood they would still embarrass me, and they did not disappoint. It took all of two minutes before Ken said to the flight attendant: "We got first class seats and we didn't have to pay for them." He kept the flight attendants busy with constant requests for food and soda, as only a boy of eight knew how. Thankfully, he was charming and the attendants, rather than finding his pestering annoying, fell in love with him.

* * *

During the next three years, Ken completed fourth, fifth, and sixth grades in Milan, Michigan. He was a member of the swim club, played Little League baseball, and participated in many activities at church.

Before their first trip to Swaziland, Dave had promised to build Ken a tree house. As is often the case with such projects, he only managed to nail down a few boards in a tree behind our house before getting distracted by the other demands of life, and his efforts lay forgotten and neglected for a time. Three summers later, something resembling a clubhouse began to take shape. With the advice of a friend and help from Ken, Dave erected a tower made out of barn wood; it was everything our children dreamed it would be. Ken, his cousin Ryan, and his sisters and friends enjoyed many hours and nights playing inside that clubhouse.

Ken and Dave working on the clubhouse

Karen Wiard
FAMILY FRIEND

Kenny was an energetic child, kind, funny and cute. He was always up to something, mostly good, something mischievous. He was full of laughter and liked joking around. His family lived in a wooded area, and Kenny loved to play outside and make forts and tree houses. I had him in my Sunday school class. and it took all he could muster to sit and listen. He was not disrespectful, just full of energy. It was always fun to have him around.

Jerri
MOTHER

Shortly before the clubhouse was completed, our dog Nicki passed away. Erica and Dave built a wooden coffin for her, and we buried her behind the clubhouse. Ken, standing by the bay window in the family room, spotted them carrying the coffin. He was heartbroken and cried for quite some time.

While our family was preparing for another, longer trip to Swaziland, we were watching one of Ken's swim meets at the Milan Swim Club. In the middle of a freestyle race, as we were cheering him on, Ken started dog paddling, waving and smiling at us. We were in the bleachers hanging our heads half in embarrassment, half in disbelief.

While he was honing his social skills in the middle of the race, rather than focusing on the task at hand, Ken was beginning to develop his athletic abilities in earnest. He was getting better at sports and becoming more competitive. Ken was enjoying getting ribbons in Swim Club for improving his times in events. He was understanding the game of baseball better, acquiring a more level swing when batting and snagging more balls in his glove. Also, by playing mostly soccer in Africa, he had really learned the game and was enjoying reliving that chapter of his life in the local youth league. Dave taught his Sunday school class for a period of time, and, for fun on Saturdays they often played some basketball and worked on fundamentals such as dribbling and passing, even learning plays here and there. Really, Ken was gaining experience in most sports available to a boy his age, and these were talents he would hone and carry into the later years of his life.

Mary Mehringer
SECOND GRADE TEACHER

I was Kenny's second grade teacher at Paddock Elementary in Milan MI. It was some years later, while eating at a local restaurant, that I was surprised and pleased when he brought his wife and new baby over to meet me.

After the introductions, I couldn't resist sharing a sweet anecdote about him that came to mind on that occasion:

It was well into winter but there had been little snow for the kids to enjoy. Having been teaching about proper friendly letter writing form, I was looking for a meaningful way for the students to practice this new skill. I encouraged them to write a letter to the weatherman requesting a good snow for sliding, building snowmen, and other such pursuits.

That night we had our first-of-the-season significant snow fall, perfect for kids' enjoyment. As the kids entered the classroom the next morning, Kenny came running up to me, grasped my arm, and blurted out, "it worked, Mrs. M., it worked"!

After much consideration, I reluctantly told him that neither the weatherman nor we controlled the weather. It felt akin to revealing that there is no Santa Claus.

Steve Gilzow
FIFTH GRADE TEACHER

I met Ken Johnson in 1980. He was a fifth-grade student, and I was his teacher. Kenny was not the biggest kid in the room, nor the smallest. Physically, he was average. But so many other aspects of Kenny were not average. What comes to mind first is his smile. He had dark eyes that crinkled during his frequent smiles, one side a little more than the other, capable of radiating pure happiness.

As I write this, 33 years after the fact, I feel I'm probably repeating comments I wrote on his report card. Kenny had that rare combination of academic and social strengths. He was one of those kids teachers pray will land in their classroom: someone who influences other students in all the right ways. He was intelligent, curious, earnest—in a word, smart—and had the knack for making those qualities contagious, because it was all framed with that smile and those eyes.

My classroom put a heavy emphasis on hands-on, experiential learning. I had a workbench in my room, with simple hand tools. The kids had to pass a test identifying the tools and showing they knew how to use them before I'd let them work at the bench. Ken was one of the first in the class to pass the test.

We built structures out of straws and pins; testing them with metal washers hung from paper clips to see how much load they would bear. From there, we finished the model at EMU, where Ken's dad, Dave, was a math teacher. It was a nice field trip and served to expose my students to college, a place I hoped they'd all end up some day. I recall Dave was able to assist us with getting precise measurements, and the careful assembly required for these activities. You could see the makings of an enthusiastic engineer in Ken.

At Christmas that year, Ken gave me an ornament he made. It is a ring of wood 3 inches across, the wood 3/8 of an inch thick, painted red, and framing an embroidered cross-stitch of my name and the year. On the back there is his neat printing, "From Ken Johnson 1980." Again, I could clearly see an engineer starting his career a couple of decades early.

Dedication to the late Ken Johnson
By: Paris Brierley

I threatened this morning that I would have to draw a picture for my One Picture, One Day, One Year series, since I cannot up load a photograph. Well, here it is.

Back in Kurt Karner's 6th grade class (that's grade 6 to all my Canadian friends), we learned about all the French explorers that explored the Great Lakes Region. Kenny, Troy Elliott and I would all sit in the back of class and take notes. Well, the three of us decided that we needed a mascot to snazz up our notes. Kenny created Pierre the French Explorer. Hmmm......now that I think of it, we should have cashed in decades before that annoying Dora cartoon. But I digress...

What ever we learned about, that week, we would draw Pierre in action poses to suit whatever situation the French explorers were in that we were learning about. it was something fun that we used to do, but it also had a collateral impact. It made it easier to skip to the section of notes we needed to study, because we could see what Pierre was doing in our notes.

Funny that after 33 years, I don't remember much about the French Explorers other than names like Cartier, Champlain, Joilet, and Marquette, but I do remember Pierre.

Jerri
MOTHER

From August 1982 to December 1983, our whole family was in Swaziland because Dave accepted the full-time mathematics advisor position at the USAID project. While there, Ken attended three different schools. At first, Ken was enrolled in Study Hall, which met at the Nazarene Mission in Manzini and was operated by Trans-World Radio.

During his time at Study Hall, one of Ken's teachers had a conference with me and said that Ken would never amount to anything because he would not pay attention and could not sit still. I remember feeling totally crushed, going home and sobbing. Never before had anyone put that to me so bluntly, with such flippant bedside manner. While I knew he had a point—Ken certainly had issues focusing and using his energy for productive ends—I was frustrated that somebody who had known my son so shortly would be so quick to write him off. As a biased parent, I thought my son had so much potential, and it hurt to hear his teacher disagree.

A while after we moved in, the kids at the mission station found a baby monkey. I've been told this was a common occurrence for the other children, but it certainly was not for mine. Naturally, they made the decision to bring it home. We nursed the monkey, fed him with a bottle and kept him warm. Unfortunately, he died a few short days later. Undoubtedly sad, it remained a great experience for my children.

Back row: Whitnie, Sonya holding baby monkey, and Ken; Front row: Erica

A few months into our stay, Ken and Whitnie moved to Pietermaritzburg, in the province of KwaZulu-Natal, South Africa, and lived with Nazarene missionary children in the One Way Home there. Ken attended Pelham Senior Primary School for boys. Most of the following year, to be closer to home, we enrolled Ken and Whitnie at Waterford International School in Mbabane, Swaziland, where ambassadors from all over the world sent their children.

Ken ready to go to Pelham Boys School, Pietermaritzburg, South Africa

Ken riding off to Pelham Boys School

The Study Hall, Pelham, and Waterford experiences certainly exposed Ken to a variety of educational systems and sharpened his ability to adapt. It gave Ken a love of the African continent, something he carried throughout his life. While he traveled limitedly on this trip, Ken's experience filled him with wonder, much like a foreign visitor to the U.S. seeing the Grand Canyon or Niagara Falls. It produced for Ken lifelong friends and exposed him to cultures far different from our own, developing in him a sense of open-mindedness that certainly served him well.

Whitnie Johnson McNeil
SISTER

During Ken's elementary school years, I vividly remember the events of his time in the seventh grade. That year, our entire family went to Africa for 18 months. My older sister, Sonya, was out of high school and traveled with the Youth for Christ Y1 program. She traveled all over South Africa with a music and drama team. My younger sister, Erica, stayed at home and attended class at Study Hall, a nearby school. Ken went to Study Hall for a very short time before the two of us shipped off to boarding school in South Africa. Because we were able to go to school anywhere we wanted, lots of prayer went into our decision to go to South Africa, where missionary children lived in a home and went to local schools. Ken went to a boy's school and I went to a girl's school, only seeing one another at home and church. I had a terrible time adjusting, but Ken, only 12 years old, would give me hugs, and tried to comfort me in so many ways.

We decided together we wanted to move closer to home for boarding school. Our only option was a school one hour from home where we would see our parents more frequently. Rumor had it they treated Americans poorly there, and we had to sit an entrance exam. As a terrible test taker, my scores were not strong enough for admission, but Ken scored high enough they accepted us both.

Acting as a sort of team, Ken supplied the brains and I supplied the brawn. Ken helped me with my studies, and I helped Ken with bullies. As I stated earlier, this school had a reputation for ugliness. We two Americans were targeted, so Ken and I often found ourselves on the defense. Even the teachers would occasionally make snide comments directed at Ken and me. When it came to other students, Ken would volunteer my pummeling services were any of the students to give him a hard time; luckily, the threat of retaliation was often enough to back them down. I did a lot of threatening during my time at Waterford, but never any actual hitting.

I remember Ken used to sleep with his jeans on with a belt and a padlock between his belt buckle and pant loop. He was scared the other children would do something to him at night when I wasn't around to help him. In many ways, we had reversed the roles we adopted in Pietermaritzburg: I was now the one comforting and giving strength to my brother. During the time I spent with Ken over that year and a half at three different schools, I watched as he quickly matured, overcoming daily struggles as he grew from a geeky little clown to a contemplative, yet still silly, teenager.

Because of circumstances I can't recall, I came back to the U.S. before the rest of my family. It was hard to leave my parents and sisters, but the hardest part was leaving my brother, who had become my best friend. I don't necessarily remember those years in Swaziland fondly, but I do see in them the seeds of the future being sown and the perspectives Ken held in later life being shaped and formed.

Kevin Wardlaw
FAMILY FRIEND

I met Kenny Johnson when I was living in Swaziland, Africa. I don't really remember how old I was, maybe 10 or 11 years old. I just remember Kenny was a bit older, and he didn't live on the Mission Station. The Mission Station was almost like our "base." Most of the missionary kids lived inside. I remember Kenny and I hit it off right away. We were very similar and liked the same type of stuff. Kenny was coming from the U.S. and he got me interested in stuff that was popular at home. I was the "African boy", and I led him on all sorts of adventures that were new to him.

One such adventure involved a snake encounter that obviously made a huge impression on him. Snakes were very common in our area, but this was definitely a memorable find. One of the snakes we have in Africa is the spitting cobra. We didn't see many cobras, and when we did, we obviously knew to stay away. One day we were at the home of one of the missionaries, exploring as usual. We came across markings in the dirt of what we knew to be the "spoor" of a snake of some sort. They would leave a pattern in the dirt that, if undisturbed, was very clear. We looked around for the snake, turning over rocks here and there, and found a family of baby snakes in a small hollow under a rock. We saw almost immediately they were spitting cobras. This put us on high alert as we knew their mother would not be far away. We kept lookout for the snake, and carefully killed the incredibly venomous babies, because they were so close to the missionary home. Nothing too dramatic happened, apart from the drama and action invented by the imaginations of young boys, but Ken was nevertheless disturbed by the experience, carrying a lifelong fear of snakes thereafter.

Dave
FATHER

This period of life was quite eventful, stimulating, challenging, and impactful for Ken. He flew on his first airplane, and left the country for the first time. He saw Christ the Redeemer statue in Rio de janeiro, Brazil, visited the Colosseum in Rome, Italy, spent time in South Africa and Swaziland, and experienced much of the world. He saw the impact of short and long-term mission projects and the larger impact of Missions across the world. Ken experienced schools in other countries, and inter-acted with people of many different cultures and backgrounds. He spent the formative years of his life doing what your typical boy would: playing sports, watching movies, going to school, and putting his expansive imagination to use. But Ken also had many adventures most people never get to have, let alone when they are children. His horizons were broadened at a young age and this fact made a huge impact on how he would see the world and his place in it.

For example, during his college years he called me sharing an idea that he had involving an interactive globe where children could place magnetized countries where they belong on the globe to help them learn geography better. We couldn't pursue the idea, but shortly after, many globes of a variety of types appeared on the market.

4
The Teen Years

Dave
FATHER

Just prior to Christmas 1983, we returned to Michigan from Swaziland, landing in New York City with all the Christmas decorations aglow. What a sight! What a season! Although we expected some culture shock prior to our trips to Swaziland and prepared the best we could for that, we hadn't expected the reverse culture shock we would experience on reentry to the U.S. after living elsewhere for nearly a year and a half. But it was real.

Since Whitnie had preceded us home by a few months to begin her junior year of high school, Ken had to adapt and manage on his own the last few months at Waterford. Shortly thereafter, he would be preparing to re-enter school in Milan, MI, at the middle of the eighth grade. At Milan Middle School (MMS), although basketball season had already begun and Ken had played very little basketball during his time in Africa, coach Karner allowed him to join the team. He became good enough to earn a letter for his performance.

In general, Ken readjusted quite quickly. His old friends and newly acquired friends at school and church were very curious to hear the many stories this somewhat "new kid on the block" had to share about his African adventures: the game parks, the huts, the crocodiles, the people, the schools, the sports, the climate, etc. The Johnson family came to be known as "the family that had lived in Swaziland."

We made presentations showing our slides, curios, and telling our stories in Ken's classroom and elsewhere. It was Ken's responsibility to show the spear and shield, the lion skin, and anything else he wished to demonstrate or talk about.

As Ken progressed through high school, he participated in a variety of sports, received the Art Award, developed into a burgeoning artist, exhibited qualities of leadership and scholarship, and continued acts of service and friendship. I will let the stories that follow speak for themselves to the caliber of man Ken was becoming.

Ken received 1ˢᵗ and 2ⁿᵈ place in his sophomore year in the area show competition for top artists from Washtenaw County schools and more. Ken's art teacher, Susan Terrall.

Jerri
MOTHER

Photography was one of Ken's many interests. During the time he was in the ninth and tenth grades, I was employed in the News and Information Services at the University of Michigan (U of M). As luck would have it, their sports Photographer, Bob Kalmbach permitted Ken to assist him on the sidelines during the U of M home football games. What a thrill it was for Ken to hand Bob lenses and other equipment and watch action pictures being taken close and personal to the Wolverines as the crowd cheered " *Go Blue*" and sang " *Hail To The Victors*." After the games they would go to the dark room and develop the recent pictures.

Ken working for Bob Kalmbach at U of M game

Ken working on U of M pictures

Also, during that period of time and in the fall of the year, Ken and Dave went deer hunting in Ohio with some relatives and friends. One of those years they hunted in Southwestern Ohio. That year Ken shot his first deer, a doe. His uncle Robert, walking along the ridge about 10:00 in the morning, had driven about six does toward Ken. Ken had his pick and chose the largest one. After he shot, he yelled "dad I got one." Dave, only 50 yards away, quickly joined him. Unknown to me, Dave and Ken hung it in our garage back in Michigan for a day before they took it to be processed. I, not having been told that it was there, walked into the garage for something and screamed louder than I ever had at any football game.

Ken and his first deer

Scott House and Ross Plasters
HIGH SCHOOL FRIENDS

Throughout our high school years, Ken was important to us. He was there to challenge us, to listen, to help when we needed it, and to support us in times of need. He was the angel on our shoulder, while we were the devil on his. Ken was the one friend who always kept us in line, but those lines were blurred on an occasion or two.

Ross Plasters
FRIEND

Ken was all about sports. All through high school, he participated in every sport he could. He played baseball, basketball, soccer, track, football, and was a cheerleader. In eighth grade, after Ken returned from his stay in Africa, he was back at MMS, where we met and became good friends, almost immediately. We liked the same things and had the same demeanor. One time during a sleepover at the Johnson's house the summer before high school, Ken challenged me to an arm-wrestling match. A Game of Arms this was not; no tickets to the gun show either. This was a case of two skin-and-bone adolescents trying to not be "girly men."

Mr. Johnson, not wanting to miss a good laugh, agreed to be the judge. After much grunting and groaning, I earned the victory. For me, this was a normal day-to-day thing, having grown up with three brothers. For Ken, who had three sisters, this was much more. From that night forward, he carried a vendetta, vowing to one day beat me in wrestling.

Ken was also a great advisor, whether he knew it or not. During our junior year of high school, Ken and I tried out for varsity baseball. Ken, forever the fierce competitor, was definitely skilled, having played his freshman and sophomore years. I only played as a freshman. Even though Ken was competitive, he was also a good friend and wanted to help me make the team. At practice, Coach Mercier told everyone to find his preferred spot on the field and try out for those starting positions.

Ken pulled me aside, talked about positions, and pointed out that he and seven others were going to try out for second base. It would be a bad idea for Ross to be the eighth. I looked around the field and noticed two or three people in nearly every position, except one. Noticing the right field position was vacant, I asked Coach Merc if anyone was trying out for it. After his quick negative, I took Ken's advice to heart, and sprinted to the grassy spot, 15 feet behind second base, and so became a starter on the varsity baseball team almost by default.

Four years after that first arm wrestle, Ken, having lifted weights and taken good care of himself, was fit as a fiddle. Ken and I, looking for something new to do, had joined the track team at the behest of Coach Pelligrini. Coach claimed we would be his "middle distance specialists" (meaning we would run the ½-mile events and relays and basically goof off the rest of the time). As one could imagine, we fully embraced it. On a bus ride back from one of our last away meets, Ken wanted a rematch. He claimed, were I to lose in front of our teammates, it would be fitting retribution for his defeat in front of his father those 4 years prior. Ken boasted he had started working out so he could one day defeat me. Never one to shy away from a challenge, I gritted my teeth and prepared for battle. I don't want to brag, but I will. I won, again, and we never talked about arm wrestling again, though we never stopped being incredibly close, highly competitive friends.

Ken and Ross

Scott House
FRIEND

Ken and I were both fast friends and constant combatants. During summers, Ken and I would practice our golf game and spent many hours at either the Hickory Woods Golf Course or at Club 23 Country Club. We would often play a round or two, as much as we could, until the sun went down. Even before we had our driver's licenses, we would ride bikes to the golf course with bags strapped to our backs. Like most sports with Ken, golf started out fun, but Ken's highly competitive nature eventually kicked in. During one match, Ken, Ross, and I were playing at EMU's Eagle Crest Golf Course. I was riding in a cart with Ken, who was driving. We were trading barbs back and forth. I can't recall who exactly said what, but as I leaned over to grab my golf ball off the course, Ken turned sharply when I was least expecting it. The next moment I lay sprawled out on the fairway with Ken laughing hysterically. I got up and chased Ken down, yelling and screaming, golf club in hand. Ken quickly sped away laughing so hard it made other golfers on the tee box look up in disapproval. For the rest of the round I rode with Ross.

Another one of Ken's favorite pastimes was being around pretty girls. You couldn't really blame him, and whether it was this motivation or the fact his basketball career was fizzling out, it made it an easy sell for our friend Marc to convince Ken cheerleading was his next sport. He took to cheerleading like a duck to water, ending his basketball career in favor of becoming a male cheerleader on Milan's co-ed cheerleading team. Ken and Marc enjoyed this so much they convinced me to join the team as well.

Along with the rigor and intense physical demands of cheerleading, we found there were many advantages linked to being a part of the only co-ed squad in the state of Michigan. One of these was spending weekends at various hotels during regional and state competitions, with the ladies not too far away. During one competition, I came down to the hotel pool to see Ken doing various cheerleading stunts with girls from other schools in the water. There were women in bikinis, water, and endless possibilities. I couldn't believe Ken's luck sometimes.

Back in the late 1980s the National Honor Society was a big deal. As the nation's only big organization established to recognize outstanding high school students, it was not merely an honor roll, but served to recognize students who excel in scholarship, leadership, service, and character. Milan High School (MHS), would have pep assemblies for the sole purpose of honoring inductees from the school. Going into that final semester as high school seniors, none of my friend group had been inducted. Somehow Ross got wind Ken was going to be inducted, so he told Marc and me to see if we could convince Ken to skip. We sold it to him as the unofficial senior skip day.

Badgered from three fronts, Ken was so close to giving in. We suggested going to Heath Beach or catching a movie at Briarwood. Despite our expert sales skills, Marc, Ross, and I could not convince Ken. At the pep assembly, we all sat together. When Ken's name was called, the look on his face was priceless: shock, surprise, joy, and then anger because his friends tried to get him to skip. As he made his way out of the aisle and toward the stage where Dr. and Mrs. Johnson were sitting, Ken whispered some choice words aimed at his friends.

After high school, I enlisted in the Army. I was discharged 3 years later as a Desert Storm hero, and, after returning to Milan, decided to go back to college. Having been away from any type of schooling for 3 years, college level math classes were difficult for me, putting it politely. Ken, the perpetual scholar, volunteered to be my tutor. Anyone who knew Ken knows he loved math. Maybe it's hereditary. After all, his dad was a professor in the math department at EMU for a number of years.

Ken and Jen were newlyweds at the time, and I spent many evenings at their house sitting at their kitchen table. Ken set practice tests for me to take while Jen cooked us dinner. Ken was always willing to share his knowledge to make someone a better and smarter person, and in my case it worked. Teaching was a natural gift of Ken's, and he had been using it long before he thought of teaching at ONU.

Scott and Ken

Ross Plasters
FRIEND

A couple years after high school, before Ken and Jen had married, I remember Ken switching majors from math to engineering. He used to say his decision was based on the story of a beautiful woman across the room. You see her, but the catch is that each time you move toward her, you are only allowed to travel half the distance between you and her. In the eyes of a mathematician, you would never be able to reach her: if you can only ever travel half the distance, half will always remain. In the eyes of an engineer, you would not only get to her, but you would lay a big fat kiss on her lips; you only needed to get "close enough." An engineer always finds a way, he'd add.

That's exactly what he did when he wanted to visit Jen over spring break at her home in Indiana. It was well before the days of GPS, so Ken had to manually plot out a course from Milan to Jen's home. Putting his great knowledge and logic to work, he laid out the route, thinking he could save time and fuel by taking country and back roads to get to Jen's house. He also decided he needed a wingman and convinced me to accompany him on this adventure.

On paper, it all looked good, but in reality, there were a number of uncontrollable factors such as cows crossing the road, tractors and combines taking up both lanes, Amish horse-drawn carriages going slower than glaciers, and four-way stops. When we arrived at Jen's house, we had burned a full tank of gas and were over an hour late. To further complicate matters, Ken, always eager to be back in the presence of his one true love, left Michigan with a scant $4 in his pocket.

Perhaps you think $4 was a lot of money back then, and it was, but the most gas someone could purchase in the early 1990s with $4 was around 5 gallons—nowhere near enough to fill up Ken's car. Learning from his previous plotting mistake, Ken decided to take the main roads and highways back to Milan. He gave Jen a hug and shook her dad's hand before grabbing me and jumping in the car.

When we were just outside Toledo, the gas gauge had sunk below the red bar. Sucking on fumes, we rolled into a gas station, where Ken miraculously pulled a credit card from his pocket. Apparently, this was a credit card only to be used for gas and only in emergencies. He had led me to believe we'd be stranded, but I guess the engineer will always find a way. I'd also wager Ken thought it would make for a better story if we didn't have to use the card, and I never had to know of its existence.

Scott House
FRIEND

All through high school and even later in life, Ken had a deep love for cars. He owned everything from a Peugeot to a red 1969 Mustang. Teaching and learning worked both ways for Ken and me. Ken was my math tutor, and I taught Ken about cars. Tutoring sessions often ended with the two of us tinkering with one of Ken's European cars. We often found the cars Ken liked to drive were way too high-tech for us to be wrenching on and we often had to call in a professional to clean up our messes.

Once, in high school, after Ken and I got a car in road-worthy condition, we decided a weekend road trip was in order. All good Michiganders refer to anything North of Saginaw as "Up North," and we decided a good destination was my parents' cabin Up North on Elbow Lake. We planned to do some fishing, motorcycle riding, and construct a fort or two in the woods.

Another road trip happened over spring break in 1988. In a newly restored European car and with $500 spending money, we pulled on our Jams swim shorts, donned our Ron Jon neon-colored Camel hats (complete with the sun-blocking back flaps) and headed to Florida. Sleeping arrangements were simple. Ken had the front seat and I slept in the backseat, bringing a whole new meaning to the word "Fahrvergnügen". Our campsite, if you can even call it such, served as the perfect spot for showing off our beach bodies and entertaining the vacationing ladies. Most of the trip was rather uneventful; it just served to further the bond I had with Ken and reinforced the important role he played in my life, just living alongside me and being supreme company.

Rev. Tom Robinson
YOUTH PASTOR

I remember Ken enjoyed doing skits for the youth ministry at our church. It was always fun to watch him in action. I have to say, sometimes I was not really sure about what he would do. He was an active leader and played an important role in helping shape the youth ministry at Ypsilanti Free Methodist Church.

Ken loved his sports, and boy, was he competitive! He played basketball for Alpha Chi, our high school ministry. The year we won the championship he could barely contain himself, he was simply beside himself with ecstasy.

We went on many youth trips, retreats, and mission trips during Ken's middle and high school years. He loved having a great time, but he also enjoyed getting serious with the Lord. I remember him having a real heart for missions even as a teen, something I'm sure began while he and his family were living in Swaziland. Being exposed to other cultures at such a young age really opened Ken's mind and heart to the different ways God worked around the globe and how readily he could use a willing person for his service.

We would meet often during his teen years, sometimes for lunch. We dialogued about many things, usually just the ins and outs of Ken's life and how he was enjoying being a teenager, but would always end talking about the Lord in some way. As a youth pastor, this is such a special thing to see because the teen years are so formative to a person's future. I caught small early glimpses of his future. When we'd talk later in his life and he would tell me stories of his present, I'd often think to myself how the things he was doing made so much sense as logical progressions of those conversations we'd had many years earlier.

Michelle Maynor Astolfi
FAMILY FRIEND

Those who spent time with Kenny will remember his wit and sense of humor—a classic Johnson trait. But Kenny was also deeply faithful, the truest friend you could hope to find, and a sincere encourager.

Our families got together for evenings of dinner and fun. When the Johnson family was in Swaziland, Kenny and I were pen pals. He even attempted to teach me a bit of siSwati in our exchanges. Our group of friends picked up right where we left off when he returned. He was universally liked, and he genuinely cared for others. Kenny was a steadfast friend.

He loved sports. He loved the competition. He was the epitome of a scholar athlete, but the thing that set Kenny apart from others was his Christian character. When we were in high school, I moved to Milan and became a member of the cheerleading team with Ken. He played a significant role in my transition from one school to another by introducing me to new friends and helping me feel welcome. We had great fun cheering together during basketball season. When I made the cheerleading team at the U of M, he continued to support and encourage me.

Kristi Svenson
HIGH SCHOOL FRIEND

Ken and Kristi

My first memories of Ken come from the school bus. I was the new kid and felt very alone, but we quickly struck up a friendship. He was always an open book, so being Ken's friend was easy.

Ken and I shared a 10-minute drive to school once he got his license. In our 10 minutes we talked about school, family, and relationships. He built me up when normal teens would be picking others apart. He shared so much: what kind of person he wanted to marry, his connection with his faith, and people for whom I should watch out. We also laughed a lot. We were not afraid to be silly. Those drives in his banana-yellow car were precious to me.

Ken was an in-the-trenches friend. I remember when I was sick with mono for weeks, Ken came and sat with me and brought treats. Sometimes he came and sat with me when I was sleeping. I still wonder if he was allowed to visit, as I was terribly contagious, but that didn't stop him. In my opinion, this was a remarkable trait of Ken's. Most friends are there for the drama when times are really tough. But Ken was always there to do his part, in the good, the bad, and the mild mundane of the in-between. He knew how to be the best of friends to those in his life, an example I learned from him and try to emulate.

Dr. Russell White
FAMILY FRIEND

Getting to know Ken as a teenager was a joy, as I found he had grown into a very bright young man who loved the Lord with great enthusiasm and wanted to serve Him with all his heart.

When I left Marquette for college, I did not see Ken for several years, however, my education brought me back to Michigan to attend medical school at the U of M shortly after I married Beth. What a pleasant surprise it was for us to discover the Johnson family had moved to Ypsilanti, Michigan, where Ken's father, Dave, was teaching at EMU. As usual, the Johnson family welcomed us with open arms, warm hearts, and plenty of good food. We spent many Sunday afternoons with the Johnson family during medical school.

By that time, Ken was 15 years old, and was a tall, lanky adolescent with his voice cracking and whiskers on his chin. Ken had such a joyous spirit, and I always enjoyed spending time with him, whether it was kicking footballs at the local high school, or golfing at the local 9-hole course. Ken was a natural athlete and always outshone me in most sports, even at that young age. I think it gave him great pleasure to beat the medical student in basketball or golf, but he was always a very gracious winner.

As Ken approached his later years of high school and was able to drive, we saw more of him. In fact, one particular summer when Beth's younger sister was visiting us, we found that Ken was visiting our apartment quite frequently. I think I was a little slow on the uptake to realize that she and Ken found each other quite interesting. Beth's sister, who was one year younger than Ken, was able to come back to Ann Arbor one other time later in the year to attend the high school prom with Ken. Ken was always a gentleman, and the two of them remained friends over the years, occasionally corresponding with each other.

Simone Iernea Goga
HIGH SCHOOL FRIEND

Ken was my goofy, fun friend who kept me on track and helped me find my way back to God when I got distracted by the world. My favorite memories are of us singing "Shine, Jesus, Shine" in the car as we drove to his parents' house where I would cut his dad's hair. Evidently my trimming skills worked well enough, as I was invited back a few more times.

Ken also let me be the first person to cut his hair and style it in art class. I told him I'd make him look so cool that all the girls would like him, and he believed me. I, of course, was praying I wouldn't mess it up and he would actually be happy with the styling in the end. After all the compliments he received from both guys and girls, I continued being his hairdresser. We'd laugh about it all the time. I even helped him find styling gel.

Ken was the guy who would always watch out for me spiritually and emotionally. If my thoughts and actions started to wander, he would pull me back and help me refocus. He'd remind me of the God we both served. He'd remind me to be the light of Christ and shine that light in the dark. He was always gentle with me, a quality that made him all the more effective and appreciated.

Ken and Simone

Carrie Roberts House
FRIEND

We made it through the perils and awkwardness of middle school and upgraded to MHS. I somehow found myself in our gang of friends: Kenny, the smart, handsome and perfectly straight arrow who never got in trouble or did anything wrong; Ross; the funny one and the basket-ball star, always cracking jokes; Scott the Jock, fun and sweet; Marc, the charming class clown; Leslie, part of Camelot of Milan; and me, a kind of misfit.

We had so many fun adventures and lived the truest form of "Friday Night Lights": good, clean fun. All the guys played football, Leslie and I were the cheerleaders, and we all met after the game for the dances and fun. Many weekends were spent playing Pictionary in Leslie's basement, tormenting the Johnson family with our loud antics, cruising Milan, and living the high school years like they were meant to be lived.

Then, during basketball season, we were invincible: a co-ed cheerleading squad where Ken, Scott, and Marc threw us high into the sky and dazzled the fans, all while cheering for Ross out on the court in his ridiculously short shorts. I'm sure the guys would hate admitting it now, but at the time, it was cool, and we were really good.

Ken and Carrie; Prom King and Queen

Senior year, we all got decked out for prom. For the first time ever, it was to be held at our high school. We arrived at the high school and the parents were all gathered to take photos, like paparazzi, and valet the cars. It was so fun. During prom, much to our surprise, Kenny and I were crowned Prom King and Queen. We were popular, sure, and Ken was a good athlete, but we weren't in the "in crowd," nor were we the most attractive. Certainly, we were surprised and thrilled to be selected together.

I remember that summer, Kenny and I were asked to ride in the parade in the Milan Fair. In typical Ken fashion, he fretted all day about what kind of car we were to ride in and be seen in, while I worried about what kind of dress, makeup, and hair style I should have. Ken and his cars; I could never understand the types of things about which he chose to be meticulous, but I'm sure he thought the same thing about me.

Ken and Carrie, King and Queen, Milan Parade

One weekend while we were all hanging out, Leslie, Kenny, Ross, and I for some reason (I still can't figure out), decided that we should make our own music video. We spent hours lip syncing and being silly filming ourselves to some New Kids on the Block song. I sincerely hope that every copy that exists of that is burned and never sees the light of day. We were ridiculously silly in that thing! Thank goodness none of us had political careers or became famous celebrities, or that thing may have come back to haunt us!!!

Linda Hulton
FAMILY FRIEND

When Kenny was a teenager, he was our son Ryan's favorite babysitter. Although his interests included sports, church events, small business adventures, and girls, Kenny always took the time to let Ryan know he was important in his life. Often when Ryan knew a church event was on the calendar, he would ask, "Is Kenny going to be there?" He knew there would be entertainment and a lot of laughter with Kenny around. In the life of a young boy, having a teen mentor and role model like Kenny was paramount in Ryan's own development into a Godly man and something for which we as parents were deeply grateful.

Ken Johnson and Ryan Hulton

Ryan's memories include hours of basketball in the church gym with Kenny's careful instructions and playful tactics. Even as a teenager, Kenny's interest in engineering was evident with Lego sets and Lincoln Logs spread out on our living room floor. Stories of the "tree house" often came up in the conversations between Kenny and his 6 year-old friend. He knew how to converse on Ryan's level and genuinely shared his caring attitude at each encounter.

Ryan enjoyed being Kenny's "sidekick" when they were both dressed up in tuxedos and mullet hair. In later years, Ryan continued to observe Ken's growth into a Godly young husband who proclaimed Jesus as Lord and loved his wife, Jennifer, deeply and completely.

Our son had just turned 31 when Ken died. Ryan has a beautiful wife and two lovely children. He is walking with God and bringing up his own family with the same character traits Ken shared with him nearly 25 years ago, including a passion for life, a strong work ethic, service to others, and, most importantly, the desire to know God deeply and intimately.

The gift Kenny gave to our family in taking the time to mentor our young son will never be forgotten, and we are extremely blessed to have called him our friend.

Gail Ray Parsons
CHEERLEADING COACH

Ken attended school with my two daughters at MHS. He was artistic and did a charcoal drawing of my daughter, Stephanie, diving. It was displayed at school and he later gave it to her. She still has it as a reminder of a true and talented friend. I was the cheerleading coach at MHS and had co-ed teams during basketball season. I could always recruit football players who did not play basketball or wrestle to be on our team as I let them do college-cheerleading type stunts and promised them I would never make them do anything that would embarrass them. Ken signed up with his good friend Scott, and we had a top-ten team in the state that year. They were really good and worked hard enough, though I think their original motive was to be with the cute female cheerleaders. Our co-ed teams were a real draw at all the games and were talented in doing co-ed stunts. Ken was always a positive role model for the other kids and I enjoyed having him on the team very much.

Ken's cheerleading; Ken is on the bottom, right-hand side

Jerri

MOTHER

Grade 12 was a year of many accomplishments and awards for Ken. He also changed direction on the sport's field. He played football, cheered on the co-ed cheer team during basketball season, and was on the track team in the spring. Dave was a statistician for the football team and always on the sidelines. The time when Ken caught a pass as a wide receiver and made a tackle right in front of him, Dave wished that he'd had a camera in his hand instead of a clipboard.

Unfortunately, Ken was injured halfway through the season, which kept him off the field for the rest of it. The ulna and radius in his right arm were separated and the arm was in a cast. The accident happened during practice the week of the game against MHS rival, Saline. Coach Robb allowed him to practice at least part of the week and had him play the role of Saline's star back so the Milan defense could practice against the "Saline offense" they would face that Friday night. At the football banquet at the end of the season Coach Robb said Ken was the best conditioned player on the team.

Ken said the co-ed cheer team he was on was the hardest sport he had ever participated in, but he enjoyed it. As a member of the track team, he was involved in several events. His best performance came as a member of the 2- mile-relay team with his friends Steve, Ross, and Pete. The school record they broke, or perhaps a sequential one, was broken about 20 years later. Coincidentally, Isaiah Fink, a member of the team who broke the record, later attended ONU and had the opportunity to meet Ken there, a school which would have significant impact on the lives of those in our family.

Although Ken didn't initially attend ONU, and there was intervening time which proved beneficial, it was ultimately the path Ken chose and how fortuitous that decision was. It brought Ken new friends, a wife, a career, and ultimately the singular opportunity that fulfilled his deepest passions and callings: teaching and missions. If he knew in high school how ONU would change the trajectory of his life, I don't think he would have believed it.

5
Spreading Wings

Jerri
MOTHER

During his high school and college years, Ken had a variety of part-time jobs including math tutoring, and working for Les Heddle at Ann Arbor Craftsmen (interior design), for Matt Cousino (custom builder), and for Cranbrook Institute in Bloomfield Hills, MI. The summer of 1991 he was contacted by his former youth pastor who asked if Ken would consider accompanying a group of Free Methodist youth by bus to Estes Park, CO, for a youth camp they would be attending. The youth pastor, Tom Robinson, said he was unable to go and Ken would be taking his place. Ken said he would do it and everything went very well during those 2 weeks.

> 06/18/88 From Ken's Log: "I'm kind of at one of my dormant stages right now. I, mean I believe in God yet I'm really not pursuing him. I still enjoy going to church, and I still love Him, yet I guess I'm just having a hard time getting excited."

Ken

During the Academic Year (1988-89), Ken attended EMU on a $1,000, 2 year renewable Art Scholarship before attending Marine boot camp the following summer. The first year of college saw Ken wrestle with the idea of his future, and while it took him time to find his footing, he was even then seeking to be faithful with the decisions he was making.

08/01/88 From Ken's Log: "I just got back from D.C. 88 last night. It was awesome! I really came to grips with a lot of my feelings about God."

Ken

Ken's Senior Picture

Carrie House
FRIEND

Ken attended EMU for his first year of college, and he and I would commute together. He had an art scholarship, and was so amazingly talented, and was studying mathematics. I still remember him doing a portrait of Leslie's sister, Stephanie, while she was diving—it was on display at our high school and was amazing. I remember Ken and his dad coming to EMU basketball games where I was cheering, as Ken was taking a photography class and had come to take photos for his project. I still have an 8 inch x10 inch glossy photo he developed in my scrapbook.

He later decided that EMU was not the place for him and he was going to change his major when he started attending ONU. I was shocked but respected his decision. It was quite a brave decision, especially when so many of us had no idea what direction we were headed.

Jerri
MOTHER

Ken stayed in good shape his freshman year by swimming and playing basketball with friends. He also worked at Imperial Sports in Ann Arbor and lived at home with us.

Just before the NCAA Basketball Tournament began in 1989, he called Dave from the store and said there was a pool for the tournament and he got Dave into it. Dave asked: "How much was it?" He said: "$10." Dave offered to pay and he said, "No Dad. It's on me." Dave was thankful but shocked. Usually, the parents do things for their college students. At any rate, there were 16 people in the pool at $10 each, for a total of $160. Each person had four teams of the 64 total. As it turned out, one of Dave's four teams was Michigan and they won that year, so Dave got $100.

During the year, one of Dave's colleagues, Dr. Joanne Coniglia, at EMU, needed an assistant for a project she was doing with students. Ken agreed to help with some experiments involving egg-dropping and other physics related activities. She said he was a great assistant.

> 12/11/88 From Ken's Log: "I've made the decision to go into the Marines. I'm really excited, yet I'm also frightened. I just pray that God will be with me the whole time, and if He doesn't want me to go then close a few doors. I feel He has been leading me to go because I feel quite a peace about it inside. My family has dealt with it quite well. I feel they will be very supportive of me. My mother started crying today in the sanctuary at church, typical mom eh?"
>
> Ken

Dave
FATHER

The summer of 1989 found Ken at Marine Boot Camp in San Diego, CA. Prior to going, he shared three excellent reasons with me as to why he wanted to be a marine, besides the fact he loved his country, which he always had. He wanted to develop his physicality further than allowed just by playing high school sports; he wanted money for college; and, he wanted to expand on his self-discipline, a skill for which Ken had begun to hold deep appreciation.

I wrote to him almost every day and continued to notice such attributes in him as leadership, administration, and service to others being developed and utilized in his life. He encouraged many of his fellow Marines by sharing with them uplifting spiritual messages from tracts I sent him on a regular basis. As squad leader, he told his subordinates what to do, and they did it. If there were issues, his management style was not one of swearing, getting upset, and yelling but one of reason and forthrightness. Through that, he won their respect. At one point, his supervisor learned Ken had certain skills, such as typing and drawing, and he was asked to assist in the office, which he was delighted to do. One day he beat his sergeant at the rifle range and that earned him the benefit of a very brief phone call home (a rare opportunity for anyone in Marine Boot Camp). He was thrilled, of course, and made it very clear in the few minutes he had to talk with us.

Carrie House
FRIEND

I went on vacation over the summer and found myself in San Diego, not far from where Ken was at boot camp. I decided I should try to find him, picked up the phone, and in a matter of a few minutes actually got to speak to him; he never ever forgot that. I still have no idea how I got through or convinced some drill sergeant he should allow me to chat with my best pal, Kenny. Now, looking back, I am thankful I didn't get him in trouble; it was darn near a miracle. He never forgot it and always brought it up when I saw him.

Once he was discharged and had come home, we took a weekend trip in his yellow convertible to visit Leslie at Taylor University. We had a great trip, and it was so awesome to see Leslie and to have that time together catching up.

Ken's Graduation from Marine Boot Camp

Jerri
MOTHER

What a thrill it was for us to fly to San Diego for Ken's graduation in August of 1989. When we got back to Michigan, he was absolutely amazed at how green the grass and leaves on the trees were, compared to the desert and southern California terrain he experienced all summer. Shortly thereafter, we took him to ONU, in Illinois, where he would room with his cousin, Ryan Miller, and become engineers together. That is where he met his beautiful wife, Jennifer Alberts. When we arrived, there was not housing for Ken and Ryan, so we stayed four days with them while they waited. Before we left, Ken met Jen at the swimming pool and told us he had met his future wife. She did become his wife and mother of his four children, but at the time, we chalked his interest up to being a lovelorn 19 year old.

Kevin Wardlaw
FAMILY FRIEND

Unfortunately, there was a long stretch of time when I lost track of Kenny. After he and his family returned from Swaziland, the next time I saw him was at ONU. Life is ironic and the world small. I was a sophomore playing on the men's soccer team, and Kenny and I became teammates. Kenny was at least 1 year ahead of me and our time together at ONU was brief. We played together for two seasons. I was a goalkeeper and he was a defender, so we saw a lot of each other on the field. We were both very competitive and had our share of heated discussions in practice and games. I will always remember how hard Kenny worked on the field. He wasn't the best player, but he always gave his full effort, a quality respected by his teammates.

I also ran track at ONU, and it was during that time I got to know Jenny Alberts. Kenny and Jenny were dating at that time and I remember being a bit jealous of him. Jenny was such a sweet and kind girl. My life was a bit of a train wreck during this period, and I remember how kind and honest she was. I look back now and see how God used her in my life. At a time when I didn't want anything to do with God, she accepted me as I was and didn't treat me any differently or look down on me like many others did. Kenny and Jenny were perfect for each other, and I could see it from the beginning. I wasn't surprised when I heard they were engaged and then married: two incredible people God put together with a purpose.

Scott McLellan
FRIEND

In all my life I had never connected with someone as I had with Ken. After only knowing him for 2 months, he asked me to stand in his wedding, something never asked of me until then, which says a lot about our friendship.

For spring break in 1993, Ken and I drove out to Milan to spend a few days with his parents, then road tripped to Indiana to get ready for his wedding, only a few months away. During this road trip, we shared life events, told crazy childhood stories, played air guitar to *Don't Look Back*, by Boston, and shared our love for the Maize & Blue!

In total, we had 20 years of friendship, and it was a friendship that didn't need to be watered to survive. Every time we saw each other, we picked up where we had left off. I haven't always done things the right way, but no matter what, Ken always supported me. He never judged me and always wanted what was best for me. I couldn't have asked for a better friend.

Mark Jones
FAMILY FRIEND

Ken and his cousin Ryan were, as an item, a singular part of my college experience. I first met them during pre-season training for cross-country at ONU in August of 1989. Ken would become an official member, while Ryan spent some time with us in training sessions in an unofficial way. I really had no idea who these guys were, and was completely ignorant of the significant shared connections we had. It would be years before I learned their mothers, who were sisters, had been good friends with my father decades ago while attending ENC.

Ken and Ryan were very close, even closer than brothers. Those who knew them understand how well they complemented each other. Ken was gregarious, outgoing, and ambitious, while Ryan was clearly the more reserved one. Ryan provided the necessary checks and balances to the relationship. Ryan was effective at calling Ken out on things if he sensed Ken was getting too full of himself or out of hand. Ryan has kind of this edgy wit he used skillfully around Ken when Ken needed a reality check. His more practical side supported and informed Ken's great ambitions.

These two men together were greater than the sum of their parts, a force to be reckoned with. On campus they did everything together and they roomed together those first 3 years. As one who has firsthand experience, if they united against you in any kind of prank, joke, or provocation, you didn't stand a chance.

It was over the course of our four years together at ONU that I got to know Ken well, and I had the privilege of tagging along with him and Ryan on several adventures. At times, Ken would lead, but just as often it was Ryan who had the plan. As the "other guy" trying to keep up with these two, it wasn't always easy, but I knew I wanted to be part of what they were doing.

I don't remember the exact evolution of the nickname I received while attending ONU. I do know it came from Ken and Ryan, and I know it originated from the 1989 movie *Indiana Jones and the Last Crusade.*

It began when Ken started enthusiastically greeting me by saying "Marcus Brody!" If you didn't know, Ken had a talent for morphing his voice to match some celebrity or well-known character. In fact, Ken's Aaron Neville impersonation singing *Don't Know Much* is a thing of legend.

I'm almost certain it was Ryan—the quieter but more mischievous of the two cousins—who pointed out the Marcus Brody character had the dubious distinction of being a little absent-minded at times. I guess they figured since I displayed similar qualities, in their eyes, I ought to be called by his name.

The short form of the nickname became simply "Brody" and it stuck. Under the impression this moniker was only used among my immediate circle of friends, I realized how very wrong my assumption was while sitting in a class next to a girl *whom I didn't even know*. The professor called my name for something to which I gave a response. The girl leaned over and questioned me in a whisper "Why did he call you Mark? Isn't your name Brody?" To this day, I am known as Brody, and I'm pretty sure Ken's sons don't even know my real name.

If there is a word or phrase that could describe Ken in a succinct way, I think "Renaissance Man" would do the trick. He was a person with wide interests, and he was an expert in several areas. Now this was, for me, something about Ken that was simultaneously attractive, fascinating, and frustrating. He was the polar opposite of my methodical temperament in so many ways, and his ability to fearlessly jump into something new and establish reasonable proficiency very quickly was impressive, to say the least.

Ken ran on the cross-country team with me his first year at ONU. I don't think he had run cross-country before, only mid-distance for track in high school. ONU was competitive enough to qualify for the

NAIA National Championships in 1989, and Ken would run for the top seven varsity squad. He would go on to compete in track and field, but why bother with distance running anymore when he had done that the previous fall? I don't know if he tried every event in track and field, but it wouldn't surprise me if he had. Long before there was Mark Hollis—ONU's NAIA and later USATF Champion—there was Ken Johnson, the pole vaulter. He placed at the NAIA district meet one year and had the plaque to prove it.

Having experienced cross-country that first year, he moved on to soccer in subsequent years and became a regular starter in the backfield, but continued with track and field in the off-season. Coincidentally, these were the years Bo Jackson was playing in both the NFL and MLB and starring in Nike's "Bo Knows" campaign. I guess you could have said that Ken was kind of a poor man's Bo Jackson.

Ken had this competitive nature and fascination with so many different things that drove him to explore as many academic, athletic, personal, and professional opportunities as humanly possible—even cheerleading, which I'm sorry to say I never witnessed firsthand. Ken never let the fear of the unknown or lack of knowledge or expertise deter him from these pursuits, and this was something about him that I loved. Having this part of Ken in my memory has helped me be less fearful, take more risks, and experience more adventure in my own life.

Jen Johnson
WIFE

It was my first day on the campus of ONU when I met Ken. I was there as a freshman, eager and excited about starting a new chapter in my life, and I knew God had much more in store. I had just ended a successful high school cross country and track career and was on the cusp of beginning my college career. That is why I found myself on campus, moved into my room along with the other fall sport athletes before the rest of the student body arrived for the fall semester.

Ken arrived early because he was coming back from 3 months of Marine Boot Camp. He had been on campus for 10 minutes when his phone rang. On the other end was the cross country coach telling Ken he heard Ken might be interested in joining the cross country team. Ken had never run cross country before, but since he just spent the summer running and marching everywhere he went, he was in decent shape, and he decided to attend the informational meeting that was happening in the Tiger Den at Parrott Convocation Center that day. I remember noticing him because he was late. He came into the meeting after it started with a handsome, but stoic face and a clean haircut, fresh from boot camp.

That weekend and the days after, as the team spent time with each other getting to know the other members, Ken and I were able to do the same, playing ping pong in the basement of Ludwig. It didn't take much time at all until we found ourselves spending every minute we could with each other. I think we fell in love in that first month we were there, and I spent the next 4 years finding out just how someone could be the coolest, yet goofiest, guy on campus.

> 04/17/89 From Ken's Log: "Lord, please send me a Christian girlfriend. I wouldn't mind waiting but if I must wait then please don't send any of these others my way."

> 05/09/90 From Ken's Log: "Well it has been a while, huh? Tomorrow is my last day of school here at ole Olivet for this year. I did quite well for this semester. I should have all As and one B (in speech). I'm not sure why I haven't written for such a long time, but I think it is because I'm in one of my notoriously dormant moods again. Hopefully this summer I'll snap out of it. My question is this: Why (like at boot camp) do I rely and trust in the LORD so much when there are hard times yet, when everything is easy, His memory fades?

> Ken

Ken and Jen in their early dating days

6
A Heart for Missions

Crystal Walls Gibbons
FAMILY FRIEND

When I think of Ken Johnson, the first thing that comes to my mind is his heart for missions. He was the first man I ever met in whom I saw a deeply seated passion to be in the mission field. Within a few months of meeting him, he was jumping with both feet into the missions program at our church. Before Ken came along, the program had been doing some good things, but it had really needed a dedicated person to elevate it. His vision was to go to one location every 6 months for 3 years, so we could make lasting connections with the people of that area as well as make the biggest impact in that community.

Having grown up spending time in Swaziland, Ken quickly started planning for the first big trip, looking earnestly for a place on the African continent where we could go. It was part nostalgia, I believe, but Ken also knew the need that persisted in so many communities all across sub-Saharan Africa. After a chance encounter with Don and Evie Gardner, missionaries living in Kenya, our destination was set.

As the plans started to come together, Ken approached me to join the team. There was a need for a video production person to go on the trip, and he thought I would be the perfect fit. His excitement was contagious, such that I couldn't help but say, "Yes." He had a way of making you feel like anything he suggested was the most brilliant idea you had ever heard.

On February 27, 2010, we boarded a plane at Detroit International Airport headed for Nairobi, Kenya. That first trip was focused on the construction of a married housing unit for Africa Nazarene University (ANU). We got to work immediately the next morning after we landed. We were working with a local foreman, whom we would come to love, named Charles Luta. He is one of the hardest working men I've ever met, and he and Ken hit it off right away. We had a great first week of work and fellowship with the local people with whom we were working. Every morning we would gather at the work site, Charles would lead us in a short devotional and prayer, and then we would get to work. After a few hours, we would take a brief tea break, which was Ken's favorite time of day, and then get back to work. Each night after dinner, Ken would call us all into his room, and we would talk about the day, share stories or testimonies we had, and pray together. He excelled at keeping us focused on the real reason we were there: to share the love of Jesus.

On March 7, 2010, after a wonderfully productive first week, we were eating breakfast and getting ready for church when six men, armed with semi-automatic rifles, came through the gates of the compound in which we were staying. They corralled us into the dining room. Through broken English, lots of swearing, and a lot of Swahili I didn't understand, they told us to lie on the floor, face down and not look up. For 20 minutes, they went from person to person, taking everything we had on us, from wallets and watches to cameras and Bibles. The scariest moment came when they started taking wedding rings. Some of the men's hands were swollen from the heat and the work we had done all week, and they couldn't get their rings off. One of them was hit in the head with the butt of a gun and began bleeding profusely. The attackers were angered at that point and started asking who our leader was. I quietly pleaded for Ken to stay put, not to speak up. The thought of any further harm coming to any of us was terrifying. After a few more kicks, bumps, and bruises they took the vans and left. The hours and days that followed were defining moments, not only for each one of us on that trip, but also for Ken as a leader and a true missionary.

After all the police reports and interviews were over, we gathered together to try to make sense of what just happened. Some wanted to go home immediately, while others thought we should stay. Ken was patient with each of us as we struggled with the decision of whether to stay or go. After all opinions had been heard, he said he wouldn't stop anyone from leaving, but he wanted us to know he didn't think God's plan for us was complete. He told us that when God's people are on the move, Satan attacks. Ken was right; we needed to stay so the people would see because we trust in the Lord we were not scared of whatever might befall us.

The week that followed was the most powerful week of missions I ever experienced. We headed out to meet the chief of a small village called Ewaso Ng'iro. He had heard about the robbery, and he wanted to meet us. Chief John Kimorgo was previously a guard in the Kenyan army, protecting the president. When we met him, he was a very serious man. He wanted to donate some of his land to us, the Church of the Nazarene, to build a church. Although he was not a Christian, he believed that we were good people and that we would build a church for his community. That day, as we sat around his yard in plastic patio chairs under the shade of his yellow acacia trees, he began his very special relationship with Ken Johnson.

Ken and Chief John were fast friends. I think John saw a little of himself in Ken. They were both great leaders; they both were very driven men, and both loved their wives and children very much. As Ken began to share with Chief John his vision for what the Brighton Nazarene Church (BNC) would do for his community over the next three years, John, too, got excited. Before we said goodbye that day, we gathered in a circle, on the land that Chief John had donated, the place we believed would someday have a beautiful church, and we prayed for God's blessing on Ewaso Ng'iro, the Kenyan people, and Chief John's family.

That trip changed most of our lives. We learned that our lives truly are not our own. God is the one who holds us in his hands, and he had a plan for each of us on the trip, including Chief John Kimorgo.

Six months passed and we kept in touch with our new friends in Kenya, but none more so than Ken and John. John would call Ken once a week and ask questions about his God, why he was doing all this, and if we were indeed returning to finish the job we had promised to do.

In August of 2010, we took a group back to Kenya. This time it was a group of teachers who were going to teach at the university. Ken's other passion was teaching. He loved learning, and seeing others learn. When the opportunity arose to teach students at Africa Nazarene University (ANU), he jumped at it. Ten teachers went on that trip and spent two weeks sharing their knowledge and experiences with the university students. For several of the teachers, it was an overwhelming and daunting task, but Ken, with his positive outlook and steadfast confidence, was sure God had a purpose for us. At the end of the second week, we took a

3-hour van ride out to Ewaso Ng'iro to visit with Chief John. As soon as we pulled in, he greeted us with a warm welcome and open arms. We again sat around his beautiful trees and talked as if we were old friends catching up after a short separation. He and Ken spent almost an hour walking the land and dreaming about the next time we would come, when we would build a church.

In February 2011, we returned and brought supplies to build the church. We started almost immediately after we landed. The team of men we brought with us was strong, and, with the help of Charles Luta and his team of local masons, the work went quickly. Every morning, people would walk by the site, heading to work, or seeing children off to school. Some even walked by with their herds of cattle and goats. After two days, as the people were headed home, they stopped and took in the building that, to them, had risen out of nothing while they had been at work that day. Word began to get out in the community that a miracle was happening. People came from all over to see the miracle. We had one man tell us he walked for five hours to see what God had done. The people were excited. They couldn't believe a week ago they had nowhere to worship, and the very next Sunday they would have a church! BUT THE TRUE MIRACLE was happening that week in the heart of one man, Chief John Kimorgo.

From the moment we stepped onto the property, he was there smiling as we had never seen before. He had a glow about him, and it was clear something had changed. He worked diligently beside us all week long. He and Ken, side by side as always, manned the cement mixer and talked for hours every day. They would stop every few hours and the three of us would make a water run. To get water for the cement, we needed to take a 5-minute, bumpy truck ride to the water hole. We used a pump to bring the water up through a hose that went about 25 feet up the side of a muddy hill into big, blue barrels. The first time we went on a water run, Ken was on the barrel duty, and the water pressure in the hose caught him off guard and water sprayed everywhere. Ken got soaked, and down at the pump, Chief John laughed and laughed. It was great fun. At the end of that first week, John told Ken that he felt God was calling him to be a preacher.

On Sunday morning, we headed to the newly built church and almost a hundred people gathered. The children came in and sang a song, the women sang and danced, and the preacher got up preached a powerful message. It was an amazing end to a great week. The building was more than the people of Ewaso Ng'iro could have imagined, but Ken thought we could do better. He wanted them to have a beautiful place to worship, not just an adequate one. For the next few days, we hunted down some matching chairs, some simple lighting, and some beautiful fabrics to decorate the front of the church. It was a chance to show the people that God cares even about the little details.

A whole year passed before we were able to return, but Ken made sure we never forgot about the people of the community or the mission. He would talk about it often and started planning for the next trip almost immediately. The plan was to build a pastor's home right next to the church, a food storage facility, and to hold a week-long Vacation Bible School for the kids of the community. On February 17, 2012, a team of 15 left Detroit and headed to Kenya to do just that.

As we drove down the path toward the village center, all the children chased after our vans. The people came out of their homes to greet us. It was clear we were no longer visitors, but were now considered family.

That trip was tough. There was so much to be done: A home and a storage building needed to be built, and a morning Bible study for women and a weeklong VBS for almost 300 kids needed to be organized. Unfortunately, everyone in our group came down with a terrible case of some waterborne illness. Even with all the challenges we were facing, Ken kept a level head and a positive attitude, which held us together. It was hard, but we finished the tasks we came to accomplish. Ken kept assuring us, just as he did on the very first trip, that God had called us here for a purpose and that Satan attacks when God's people are doing good.

As we got into the vans to leave and Chief John said goodbye with tears in his eyes, calling us brothers and sisters, we knew God had blessed our efforts over the last 2 years. We had all been changed by the work God had done here, but none of it would have been possible without the vision and passion of Ken Johnson. He had the heart of a true missionary and taught each of us how to find that within ourselves.

Pastor Ben Walls
PASTOR, BRIGHTON CHURCH OF THE
NAZARENE, BRIGHTON, MI

A few years ago, our church was asked to help with a church plant not far from us. It turned out that it was a church plant Ken and his family were helping get started. They had moved their home to this new location to help start the church. It was obvious to me what a wonderful family the Johnsons were, and it was during those days Ken and I started a friendship for which I will be forever grateful.

Ken and Jen's calling for missions was so real to them; they had sold their home and were renting to eliminate expenses, preparing for whatever God was about to do in their lives. Ken's heart bled missions, so we asked Ken to lead our Missions Department at Brighton. Ken quickly organized it into three levels: local, regional, and global. He put leaders into place and led the team into a great season of work and growth.

Ken and I would often have lunch together simply to talk over Kingdom concepts and ideas. I would always leave those talks amazed at Ken's insights and perspectives. The more time I spent with Ken, the more I understood the love he had for God. Ken was one of the most outstanding churchmen I've ever met. My life and my ministry have been enriched because of my friendship with Ken, Jen, and their kids.

Andrea Richardson Samuelson
CLASS OF 2013

Professor, engineer, manager, leader, and missioneer - all of these titles can be used to sum up the professional legacy of Dr. Ken Johnson. I would like to add another dimension to this list as my contribution to his memory—counselor. Dr. Johnson not only demonstrated strong leadership characteristics, but he also showed wisdom through his advice.

I had the privilege of going to Swaziland, under the leadership of Dr. Johnson, with a missions team from ONU. While on this trip, I was wrestling with some very crucial life questions, as I had just completed my senior year. I was facing a summer of decisions—what career would I choose and where would it lead me? What role should missions play in my life? Should I enter into a new relationship? I was open and ready for God to lead me anywhere, but I was still anxious, hesitant, and scared.

Toward the middle of our trip, I was having a conversation with a couple of girls on our team. We were discussing some of these important questions, particularly our thoughts on the dating relationships we were facing. Dr. Johnson must have overheard our discussion because he soon joined us. We talked with him for around an hour on what Godly relationships should look like. He took the time to counsel with each one of us individually by asking what kind of men were in our lives and whether the relationship was God-honoring. He gave us such wisdom and perspective that only comes from many years of marriage.

We were incredibly touched by the way that he talked about his wife, Jen. It was obvious they had built their marriage on solid Biblical principles, striving to put each other's needs before their own. Dr. Johnson shared with us the story of how he met Jen and some stories from the time they dated. He used those stories to give us advice on how to build strong relationships. Personally, he showed me the importance of praying for my future spouse. I remember being encouraged with the thought of the blessings that could come from consistent prayer for a particular person. Dr. Johnson showed me, through his testimony and counsel, that praying for someone fervently and whole-heartedly would take our focus off our selfish desires and could make the path clearer in regard to future decisions.

Following that evening of discussion, I was more aware of how Dr. Johnson led our team as a father figure. He provided gentle direction and care in a way that made everyone feel unified and appreciated. He seemed to have a sense of the exact type of encouragement that each person needed. Whether he was praying with an elderly lady with HIV or simply having an informal chat with our team, we consistently saw the Holy Spirit at work in his life in Swaziland. I began to understand from his example that, even though missions can and do happen overseas, outside the context of our lives, we are constantly acting as missionaries, even amongst our friends and family. Everybody can use the Gospel. It is good news for a reason, and Dr. Johnson lived in a way as to serve a constant reminder of the Gospel.

Ken praying with a lady in Swaziland, Africa

Don Gardner
EAST AFRICA FIELD STRATEGY COORDINATOR

Ken Johnson's heartbeat was for missions. He loved being "on the ground" in Africa, working among the people. Ken's rare gift for connecting with people would open the door for him to share Christ. His greatest strength was his ability to easily develop friendships across cultures and with whomever he came into contact. Ken's great love of the Lord and his Christlike commitment were obvious to anyone who came to know him.

We first met Ken in the Detroit Airport. He had just arrived on another flight and was waiting for us at the top of the jetway so he could take us to meet Pastor Ben and other church leaders who would bring Work and Witness teams to Kenya.

Ken brought the first Work and Witness team from the BNC to Kenya to work on the construction of married student housing for ANU. Thus we began a heartwarming relationship that carried us together over the hills of Michigan and the savannas of Africa. Ken's enthusiasm and commitment to missions led us into a 5-year partnership with BNC, a partnership that would make a major impact on Nazarene missions in East Africa

Under Ken's leadership, BNC provided food relief during drought, built and planted a church, parsonage, and a food-bank storage warehouse in Ewaso Ng'iro, Kenya. And while he mixed concrete, Ken led Chief John to the Lord. Their conversation began with the circumstances in which the Lord moved Ken's church to come to Kenya. John asked many questions, and one day Ken led him in the sinner's prayer and John gave his heart to the Lord. Ken stayed in contact with John, even while back in the US. Through many phone calls and emails, Ken continued to disciple John, who felt called to be a pastor. John now leads the Ewaso Ng'iro Church of the Nazarene.

John Kimorgo
CHIEF OF EWASO NG'IRO, KENYA

Ken was an amazing man; he was such a kind person with whom you could relate well as he got to understand you better. He really meant a lot to my family and me. Ken wanted my son, Ariel, to come and live in the U.S. Ken was a person with high integrity who was intelligent, humble, and loving, all with a sense for humanity, a true servant of God. Though our time together was short, he remains my absolute mentor. He left behind a legacy of hope and fame to us all in the Ewaso community. We will remember him always.

Ken and Chief John

Taylor Williams
CLASS OF 2016

Most of the memories that come to mind when I think of Babe Ken (Bah-bay) involve being on a missions team with him in Swaziland and his attitude toward missions, in general.

I want to have the same drive Dr. Johnson had: He saw a need and wanted to fix it, no matter what. His heart for missions helped to shape my own. I plan to do long-term missions with engineering, and he's helped shape what that will look like. He was the first to really encourage me in that area. I remember meeting him and talking to him the first time when I introduced myself to him for the Swaziland trip. I just walked away feeling very encouraged by his attitude. When I considered transferring, he made me want to stay at ONU because of the passion he had for engineering and for helping people.

Rose Timbers Crane
FAMILY FRIEND

Ken Johnson dropped by his parent's home to greet my husband, David, and me one night in November 2011. We exchanged greetings, caught up on family news, and enjoyed a long visit before the conversation turned to one of Ken's greatest loves: missions. Ken shared with us his love of places in Africa he'd been and the work his team was doing in Kenya. David told Ken that going to Kenya and working with the children was my lifelong dream. Instantly, Ken invited us to join the team he was leading in February, which would include two building projects, and a week-long Bible school for the children of the village. My entire being quivered with excitement, but then the doubting set in. It was so soon. We had little time to create the budget. My grandchildren needed me here.

After much discussion, Ken turned to me and said, "The one thing I would say to you is, if you want to go to Africa, do it now. You and Dave would be great assets to the team. Why wait? Do it now. There will always be reasons why another time might be better. This is your lifelong dream. Don't wait; do it now. Discuss it, pray about it, and give me a call."

Ken was absolutely sure God had set this night up in full detail to offer us the opportunity to serve in Kenya with this BNC team. He was equally sure the right answer was to do it now. Ken, in true Ken fashion, was positive, inviting, and contagious. His words of advice played over and over in our minds and in our conversation over the next week. David and I decided Ken's advice to do it now outweighed all our reasons to wait for another trip at a later date.

We joined the team on the trip to Ewaso Ng'iro in February 2012. The trip and the work was a dream come true. Ken Johnson touched our lives very deeply with his love and leadership. Because of Ken, we will more often "do it now." Through Ken's life and his death, we understand the window of opportunity to serve can indeed be very short. I can still hear the words "why wait?" that Ken would often say to each of us.

Janet Boomer
FAMILY FRIEND

I answered the call to missions in 2010, for the February 2011 trip to Kenya. I was planning on spending time at Tenwek Hospital because of my background in healthcare. I had been attending church on my own since 1995 and had been praying for my husband Pat since that time. When I told Pat I was planning to go to Kenya, he said he wanted to go with me—not because he was interested in missions, but because he wanted to be nearby if anything should happen to me.

I was frustrated with his reasoning for the trip. For me, our marriage was not in a good place, and I had been contemplating leaving Pat. When I told Ken about my husband's interest in going, he was enthusiastic but said he had to meet with Pat to get a measure of his character since he was not attending church. I know Pat was a little nervous, but he met with Ken at a local diner in Howell. Pat instantly felt at ease with Ken, and I was happy Ken vouched for Pat's character in order for him to be part of the mission team.

On the day of departure, we arose early to finish packing, and Pat went to get his hair cut. By the time he got home, he was vomiting and had become very ill. I finished packing while Pat lay in the fetal position on the living room floor. Pat later said he came very close to not going on the trip. I was able to get him comfortable with some medications, and he slept the entire way to Kenya. We spent the first couple days together, and then Ken drove the medical team to Tenwek Hospital in Bomet,

Kenya. At that point, Ken and Pat became roommates for the remainder of the time spent in Ewaso Ng'iro. We reunited at the end of the trip for the safari in the Maasai Mara. It was then I told Pat I was considering leaving him. We sought counseling with my pastor upon our return, and Pat started attending church with me.

When planning for the next trip to Kenya started, I signed Pat and me up to attend. Deep down in my heart, I knew it wasn't the right thing to do, but Ken was super enthusiastic and wanted us to go again. At the end of September 2011, I came down with a severe bout of pneumonia and was hospitalized for 8 days. I was put in isolation because of my previous trip to Kenya. Doctors were worried I had contracted something nasty during my trip. I refused all visitors, and spent a lot of time talking and crying out to God. I also wrestled with God over my stubbornness and unwillingness to give up the second trip to Kenya. Because of the nasty diseases I could have possibly contracted in Kenya, my blood was sent to Mayo Clinic for testing. My doctor informed me it could be 3 or 4 more days before results came back. I wasn't going to be released until they knew I wasn't a health threat to others. That night, I finally let go and told God I wouldn't go to Kenya. The very next morning, the doctor walked in, told me my results came back, and that I could go home. I knew then that God was waiting for me to surrender and give up on going back to Kenya. When I told Ken we wouldn't be returning to Kenya next year, he was clearly disappointed.

About 6 or 8 weeks before the 2012 trip was to depart, Pat and I exited the sanctuary at church and saw Ken at the missions booth. We walked up to say hello, and Ken immediately said how he could really use Pat on this trip because he was short on men. I looked up at my husband to see tears fill his eyes. He instantly said, "Yes" to Ken, but he caught himself, looked at me, and said to Ken that we needed to discuss it first. It was awkward and funny, but somehow I knew from whence my husband's desire was coming and there was no way I was going to stand in the way of God moving in his life. I immediately gave my blessing on the trip. Pat later told me that he told God if he was to go to Kenya again, the mission team would have to ask. He wasn't going to volunteer.

It was this second trip that completed a transformation in my husband. Again, Pat and Ken were roommates. Pat returned from Kenya a spiritually transformed man. He has taken a spiritual leadership position in our home, and looks to God in his daily life. Our marriage has been transformed and has a depth to it that wasn't there before. Pat spent nearly 30 days in total with Ken, most as Ken's roommate. I marvel at how I prayed for almost 15 years to have a spiritual partner in my husband, got to the point of giving up on my marriage, and God used Ken during two, 2-week trips to Kenya to facilitate huge changes in my husband. If God had not removed me from the second Kenya trip, Pat would not have been Ken's roommate, and the outcome could have been completely different. I think God allowed Pat to be ill during the first trip, to humble him and prepare him for the second trip. God allowed me to become ill before the second trip in order to get me out of the way so Ken and Pat could be roommates again, and God could complete His work in Pat.

I don't understand how God works sometimes, why certain people depart this life seemingly too soon. I do know, however, that Ken's years were spent well, if only he managed to witness to my husband. Fortunately, his life affected far more than just my marriage-- his impact was as deep as it was wide, and he served to inspire the best in me and my husband as we wrestled with our service for God's kingdom.

Cindy Wines
EASTERN MICHIGAN DISTRICT PRESIDENT,
NAZARENE MISSION INTERNATIONAL

It was a privilege to know Ken. We became acquainted with each other through what I believe was God's direction. The Eastern Michigan District in the Church of the Nazarene was planning a Work and Witness trip to the Philippines to work on a project for Asia Pacific Nazarene Theological Seminary. We were joining other districts from our region to help complete the project within three years. When we were in the beginning stages of our plans, the coordinator for the project resigned from the District, leaving us without a leader. Thus I set about trying to find someone to fill this spot.

It was at this point I was introduced to Ken. He was highly recommended to me by several individuals. I contacted Ken, and he was willing to help us lead this effort for the District. As we talked, he shared with me his involvement in missions at his local church. There is no doubt he loved God and loved being involved in anything that would help reach others with the Gospel. He also shared that his in-laws had just returned from the Philippines after working on this same project. What a perfect guy he was going to be for this job!

As part of his District responsibility, he was asked to attend the council meetings. His passion and creative thinking were very helpful to us. Ken even taught us how to use Facebook at one of the meetings. I know, to much of the millennial generation, that is something to laugh about, but for a missions organization comprised mainly of individuals who typed papers on typewriters, understanding a modern outreach tool like Facebook was a serious step. We loved having him as part of our Nazarene Missions International council.

Ken started with the plans for the trip. Before long, Ken informed me he had accepted his position at ONU and would have to resign his position. We were sad to see him go, but we knew even the short season he served with us would prove fruitful in our efforts.

Dr. Russell White
FAMILY FRIEND

I didn't see Ken for quite a while after he graduated from high school. Beth and I moved to Providence, RI, where we would stay for 6 years while I completed my residency training in general surgery, and then we moved to England where I studied cardiothoracic surgery. We saw the Johnsons only occasionally during that time, and Ken was usually away at college. We felt the Lord leading us into full-time medical missions, so in 1997, we moved our family of three children to Kenya to begin work at Tenwek Mission Hospital, where we have remained to this day. During our home ministry assignments in the U.S., we traveled through Ypsilanti to speak at the Free Methodist Church, and we stayed with the Johnson family in their new home in Milan, Michigan. We enjoyed many warm summer evenings in their swimming pool, where Ken was always the life of the party with back-flips and cannon balls into the water. It was a great joy to eventually meet Ken's new wife, Jen, and later spend time with all their children.

Ken strongly felt the pull of the Lord to be more involved in direct outreach with the Gospel to the world around him and began going out on mission trips with Work and Witness programs through his local Nazarene church. Ken and I talked many times about how the Lord might use him and Jen, possibly in full-time missions work. One of these short-term trips brought Ken and Jen to Kenya to work on a mission building project for the Maasai people, within about a 1-hour drive of our hospital. They were able to visit us several times over the following years, and Jen even stayed in our home and took care of our children for a week while Beth and I had to travel unexpectedly. Jen was also able to contribute to the work at Tenwek with her skills as a physical therapist.

During one of their trips to Kenya, I distinctly recall Ken calling me to tell me most of the members of his team had been struck with a gastrointestinal illness that kept most of them away from the work site, preferring to stay close to the hotel where they were staying with its toilet facilities. I made the drive to pay house calls to many members of the team, and was blessed with gifts of stool samples from several team members. I brought one team member back to Tenwek for rehydration, but all the others seemed to be on the mend with some oral antibiotics. Ken was the leader of the team and made sure everyone was well taken care of.

Ken had a sharp mind and a unique ability to look at complex problems and develop clear, manageable solutions. Others looked to him as a natural leader, and his infectious humor and good nature drew others to him. I always wondered where the Lord might lead Ken and his family in the future, as I knew that Ken was very much seeking the Lord's will with a great desire to serve Him for the greater good of the Kingdom.

Aaron Lucas
CLASS OF 2013

One of the coolest interactions I had with Dr. Johnson was during missions week at ONU. On my way to lunch, I saw him standing by the Swaziland table. I honestly wasn't interested in going, but because I had a lot of time before my next class, I decided to stop by and say hello. What I thought was just going to be a short conversation turned into a 45-minute discussion about engineering-based missions. It was one of the most engaging conversations I have ever had. It was from that conversation with Dr. Johnson that God started revealing to me my own desire for missions.

I don't know if Ken ever knew the impact that conversation had on my life. Because of that conversation, I decided last minute to apply for the Swaziland trip. I will never regret making that decision to apply. As I think back about all of the interactions I had with Ken, I cannot think of a single one where I didn't see him living his life for Jesus. Even when he and Luke, his youngest son, got left behind in Swaziland, he seemed to stay very calm and collected, and if he was mad, he did not let it drag him down. Instead he just kept on doing exactly what needed to be done.

Jen Johnson
WIFE

It seems Ken always had a heart for missions. Specifically, I think God placed in him a love for the African continent, starting when he was there as a kid. Separate from the life I enjoyed with my husband, I had a rich missions legacy from my parents going on yearly Work and Witness trips as far back as I can remember.

Long-time friends of Ken's family are currently working as medical missionaries in Kenya, and every time they were on furlough, Ken and I made a point to meet with them to talk about Kenya and the amazing things God was doing there. It wasn't long after one of these visits where we heard their stories that Ken began to wrestle with a call that God was putting on him. I remember he had been very quiet and introspective when, after about a month of this internal struggle, he turned to me one night, and said, "I think God wants me to go into full-time missions." I remember clearly responding with a "Really?" and then with an unimpressed "huh." In the next couple of months, though, I began to see God was calling us to action to make missions more central in our lives. The entry in Kenny's Log, as he called it, on August 19, 2004 stated: "I feel a call from God to shift into some type of full time ministry in about four years (either teaching or missions)." There were many seemingly huge obstacles in our way before we would be free of the financial anchors holding us down, but with God all things are possible, and it was an amazing journey from the moment we both said, "Ok, we will."

At that point in our lives, we were what some would call "house poor." We had our fair share of nice things: a big house, cool cars, and other toys. We were in debt to our eyes and we knew we would forever be chained to this debt unless we took huge steps to get out from under it. First things first, we signed up to take a Bible-based debt reduction class. Not only did we take the course, but we also turned around and taught it twice to friends of ours and began to follow the principles, looking at money and possessions in a completely new way. All things belong to God; we had things only because God had seen fit to bless us with those things, and debt was bad.

Soon after, we heard about a different course, one from the well-known financial author Dave Ramsey. After taking it ourselves, we signed up to teach this course as well. By this time, we had sold our Corvette, after having owned it for only 18 months, and used the principle of the snowball to take care of a lot of our credit card debt. God was blessing us right and left with bonuses from Ken's job, many of which were a "surprise" and not planned.

We also signed up to take the Cross Cultural Training course from the Church of the Nazarene. This was a course that all who were interested in going to missions were encouraged to take so we could find out our strengths and better align with our call. Not surprisingly, Ken had many strengths in the area of fundraising, administration, and people. My strengths were more in medicine and compassion.

Ken continued to be blessed with new and better opportunities in his job. He also was having opportunities to share his faith at work, something for which he would eventually get in trouble. He worked with a very diverse group including, among others, a Catholic, a Jew, a Buddhist, and an Evangelical Protestant. He never came out and spoke directly about his faith, just always lived it out in his actions and words of caring, and with joy. He was known for his integrity. One day, he went to work and noticed the Buddhist was there and very unhappy. Ken asked him what was wrong and he relayed to him that his wife had just miscarried their first baby. He was very saddened, understandably, but when he spoke about it, he also shared that he and his wife felt it was their fault in some way because of Karma; perhaps in some former life they had done something bad and this was retribution. Ken felt compelled and shared with him his faith in a God who loves and is gracious and forgiving. He planted seeds of faith in that co-worker's heart and Ken never passed up an opportunity to ask about his coworker's faith and traditions. He found a way to relate to that man along with the others with whom he worked.

Soon after, his superiors, in their routine yearly employee review, did a 360-degree co-worker review. At that time, someone complained that Ken spoke too much about his faith. He was given his raise, but was warned not to speak again about his faith at work . That did not sit well with Ken, and he wrestled with it for about two weeks before something happened that can only be described as God's deliverance. Ken was in the airport coming home from yet another business trip, a reality he was beginning to lament and of which he was quickly tiring. He was walking in the airport and he heard someone shout his name: "Ken, Ken Johnson, over here!" He looked and saw a familiar woman, someone with whom he once worked on a project at Ford Motor Company, waving her arm in the air to get his attention.

Dawn was her name, and she was so excited to see Ken. She had recently left Ford to create her own company called Solidica. She was excited because she had been looking for someone to hire with specific qualities to help her grow the company, qualities she knew Ken to have through working with him previously. One such quality was his talent to brainstorm and come up with ideas. Not only could he come up with ideas, but he was also able to come up with a plan to carry them to fruition. He came home after that and shared with me the opportunity, however risky it was, to go to work for Dawn. On the spot, she offered him a position as Vice President for Development, and in 2 weeks, after we both prayed about it, he accepted the job. This new job and new company would bring him the opportunity to flourish as an innovator and collaborator. It also gave him the deeply fortuitous opportunity to earn his Doctor of Philosophy (PhD).

His lifelong love of learning never left him, and having the opportunity to get his PhD fulfilled another objective. This would give him the credentials he needed to teach someday at the university level, something he was certainly keen to do. During this time, we had continued to eradicate debt and felt this new job was another blessing from God. Not yet knowing how this call to missions would take shape, we continued to study and soak up what we could learn about Kenya and Africa, in general, meeting with our medical missionaries serving in Kenya every chance we got. While Ken was working at Solidica, earning his PhD and getting promoted, he was also given the opportunity to serve as the Missions Director at BNC.

"The Naz," as it was affectionately called by attendees, was a church of about 800, and very missions-minded. It just needed a person to direct it and push it forward to accomplish a goal. BNC had a pretty good grasp on local missions, having built an indoor skate park for area youth to enjoy, and by developing the biggest Celebrate Recovery groups in the state of Michigan. So when Ken became the Director, he devised a plan to have the Missions Department encompass local, regional, and global dimensions.

He placed people to lead the local and regional arms of the plan and took on leading the global aspect of missions for BNC. He started working on possible places for Work and Witness teams to be able to go. At first, he started working with another church on the district that needed a partner to go to France to work a long term 5-year plan with a specific church and town over there. He was not overly excited about it, but he was willing to pursue and learn what he could about that opportunity. He and I were a bit disappointed because we felt like God had led him to this position as a way to reach the people of Kenya. We went forward with it for about 2 months.

Things were not going well in the planning stages, however, and suddenly the France opportunity fell through. In the same breath the lead person used to tell Ken France was no longer on the table, mentioned this small village called Ewaso Ng'iro, in need of food and water supply in Kenya. Immediately, Ken's heart began to beat wildly and we knew God was moving once again. No one on the team he served on knew of Ken's love for Kenya. Was this what God's call was? To serve the people of Kenya from America? Regardless, we suddenly were sure we would be going to Kenya, if only for a couple of weeks at a time. And soon!

Ken began working on relations with the Chief of the little Kenyan village of Ewaso Ng'iro and also with the Regional Directors of the Eastern Africa District, Don and Evie Gardner. Soon, we found ourselves, along with fifteen others from Brighton, on our way to Kenya. This trip would accomplish a couple of things: we would spend 10 days working on married housing for students of ANU, and we would meet with the chief and tour the village where we would eventually establish a four-or five-year partnership.

In the end, it brought fresh water and food to people directly affected by serious drought. A food storage unit, a church, and a parsonage were also built over the course of the time we invested in Ewaso Ng'iro. We also were able to form strong friendships with the chief and his family, the pastor of the church and others in the village.

Bob Kennedy
FAMILY FRIEND

I recall being at a New Year's Eve party that one of the people at the NAZ was having and Ken was there. I overheard him talking to someone about missions. Something about this conversation caused me to want to hear more. Later that night, if I was close to Ken, I would be sure to listen to what he was saying. It always seemed important. He spoke of possibilities and of REAL contributions--not the kind of things that others might do but things about which he had knowledge beyond his years. I would say he was truly God's man.

My past life experiences had always led me to find that people who sounded like this were mostly unapproachable, but something about Ken made me want to speak with him directly. One of the conversations he was having was about different religions and belief systems. He again spoke with such authority, yet not in a way to lower the self confidence of anyone who was listening. In fact, what he said seemed to challenge me to know or do more in my life.

I had a chance to talk with him for just a few minutes that night, so I asked him how he knew so much about other beliefs and religions. He said it was just part of the curriculum when he was in college. I told him I didn't think I got that same detail though I attended a Christian college. Even though I had not grasped these concepts as well as he did, he was very generous in his spirit toward my lesser understanding. I sensed a true Christ--centered spirit in him. When our conversation ended, I felt motivated to know more and blessed to have had a chance to see Ken's heart. He was truly a man of God and was showing that in action in the Kingdom's work.

It was more than a privilege to know Ken and to talk with him for a few minutes. It was an inspiration for me and how I live my life. I will always remember Ken's confidence in God and the work that he was doing for God while on this earth. But even more, I will remember how generous his spirit was to someone interested but not as knowledgeable as him.

I consider myself blessed to have known him.

7
Professional Life

Dr. Johnson held two patents, was the recipient of numerous industry awards, regularly presented at international conferences and expositions, and published articles in multiple scholarly and industry journals.

Dave
FATHER

Ken had a dream, a dream planted in him in Swaziland when he was a young boy. This dream would become his ultimate goal: to work the missions full time and support and educate his family.

Ken walked a ways to get there. Early in that walk, shortly after college, he established a business, Milan Sports Connection, in downtown Milan. He envisioned it as a fun, safe, and wholesome place for kids in Milan to hang out. His mom rented a separate section of that store for a business she owned, Weddings with Care. Incidentally, only a block away was City Hall where a charcoal drawing of downtown Milan hung that Ken had drawn during his high school years. He told us that he learned more by forming, owning, starting, and running a business than he ever learned in school. In the meantime he moved up the corporate ladder, through the perks and around the inevitable debt that came with high-flying positions. He spent years, nearly two decades, working as an engineer in various capacities and at multiple companies, some of which he owned, racking up the accolades and experience that would uniquely qualify him for his position at Olivet. That position, in many ways, would fulfill

Ken's dream and allow him to be an engineer, teach, raise a family, and make a steady impact for the Kingdom through missions.

His contribution to the engineering field and his business acumen was clear throughout his career. We knew about the risks he might have to take, the big projects, and the awards. Ken could never think small, so this was the natural progression of his life. His enthusiasm for new things knew no bounds. To Ken, nothing was impossible.

Through the memories of the people he worked with, however, we came to see that, indeed, business was never just business with Ken, and while we knew quite a bit about his work, what we knew was only the tip of the proverbial iceberg.

Jen Johnson
WIFE

We had many adventures while we were at ONU. We knew we would be married one day, and many people advised us to wait until we were finished with school to get married. So, we got married one week after we received our degrees from ONU, and we moved to South East Michigan where he and I spent the summer teaching gifted middle school students at Cranbrook Institute. We were part of a program that gave extra educational opportunities to students from inner-city Detroit who showed promising futures in the areas of science and math. This was one of many times when I saw just how much Ken loved teaching.

Ken and Jen's Wedding Picture

4-8-93 "I just graduated from ONU. I'm not sure what I am doing next summer yet, but, I'm excited about the possibilities. Thank you Lord for bringing me here."

Ken

He eventually found a job in Ann Arbor, and we settled down in that area. He was a quick learner and had an entrepreneurial mind that worked well for him in the engineering and business world. He had an opportunity to earn his Master's degree from the U of M. God blessed him with that opportunity, paid in full by the company for which he was working at the time. The company was so impressed they also allowed him to pursue a doctoral degree in manufacturing and engineering. He was a gifted learner and was always interested in doing more in the classroom.

In the meantime, I was also pursuing my dream of becoming a Physical Therapy Assistant (PTA), working my way through the program into which I was accepted. It was while I was finishing these classes that I became pregnant and had a little girl. I finished and went to work part-time as a PTA in the evenings when Ken could watch Sydney. I continued to work, and we soon had two boys, Erick and Luke, at home with Sydney. When I was pregnant with our fourth child, we decided that I needed to stay home. God blessed us with these children, and he also made a way for me to stay home with them while Ken went to work for Delphi and eventually for Solidica.

Ken was very busy as well during this period, as he was continuing his classes toward a doctorate, and coaching a high school soccer team. After Bethany, our fourth came along, I was very busy at home, and it became apparent I needed help with the kids. I remember one time when, after a particularly crazy stressful day, I sat on the steps by the front door of our house with the keys in my hands, waiting for Ken to get home so that I could get out of there to have some time to myself. Looking back, I am sure he probably had just as hectic of a day, but all that mattered to me was getting out of the house for a spell! After I came back later that evening, I found him with the kids in the family room, playing and having a great time. He loved his kids, and he loved being a dad. It wasn't long after this he decided to drop out of the doctoral program at the U of M so he could be home more to help me during that hectic time while the children were so small.

Ken and I became very involved in our church, specifically with the college-aged ministry. Since we lived and went to church in a college town, our church had an opportunity to minister to those who were in the area while they were students. We led a Sunday school class and also had a chance to mentor college-aged couples. Ken had a unique way of helping and encouraging them, and we became lifelong friends with some of those couples who had been there as students.

While we were continuing to stay busy in our church's ministries and missions, Ken changed jobs and became an executive in the patents department at Delphi. He was enjoying this new challenge but found the job and the bureaucracy of a large company to be stifling for his entrepreneurial mind. However, he worked as he always did: for the Lord. He also found himself working alongside a religiously diverse group of people that Ken was able to ask about their religious beliefs. He became very curious and wanted to learn more about them. It was then that we started a new Sunday school class that focused on learning about the different cults, sects, and religions of the world. He felt this was the best way to learn about them himself. He also wanted to be able to converse with his co-workers on a deeper level and understanding, bridging the gap of differences between them.

In addition to the discussion with his Buddhist friend I noted earlier, Ken had similar conversations with his other co-workers, including a Jewish man, a Catholic, and a Muslim. What Ken was teaching in our Sunday school class about the world's religions gave him a new understanding of their beliefs and helped form a more personal relationship along with their professional relationships! He never forced his faith on them, but he certainly had many conversations with them, asking questions about their beliefs.

Those early years of our marriage certainly were tumultuous. We experienced a lot of life together, Ken and I. Through new jobs, four children, newer jobs, moving, finding our place within the Church, and navigating the different calls God put into our lives, I am so thankful Ken was there with me through it all. We encouraged each other and supported the decisions we made as a couple, doing our best to faithfully serve the God who brought us together before our freshman year of college officially started.

Jerri
MOTHER

I was the Vice President of an employment agency and had gotten Ken a temporary job at the National Center for Manufacturing Sciences (NCMS) in Ann Arbor, MI. He worked in that position for 3 or 4 months when a permanent position opened. I submitted his résumé and the résumé of one other candidate. The other candidate looked impressive on paper, with many years of experience. By comparison, Ken's position looked hopeless; he had no work experience in the engineering field and was fresh out of school. Yet, miraculously, the folks at NCMS gave me a call and said they would be hiring Ken for the position.

Ken's first job was as the Technology Sourcing project assistant at the NCMS. He was responsible for identifying high-potential advanced technology candidates who qualified for further development and commercialization from across the globe. During this time, Ken collaborated with organizations in Russia in conjunction with the U.S. Department of Energy and companies such as Ford Motor and General Atomics.

In September 1994, he was promoted to Advanced Manufacturing Technology program manager, managing several collaborative industrial research projects. It was during this time Ken met David Tait.

David Tait
FAMILY FRIEND AND COLLEAGUE

I met Ken almost 20 years ago when he was a program manager at the NCMS. NCMS is an entity funded by the Department of Defense with the purpose of bringing government and industry together to collaborate.

Collaboration was in Ken's DNA. I called him and he asked me to come and present what we were doing, using rapid prototyping models to produce epoxy molds for plastic injection molding. Ken introduced my company, Laser Form, to his team of Pratt & Whitney, Baxter Healthcare, and some folks from Texas Instruments. They approved us joining the team.

Personally and professionally, this was huge. I choked up when Ken informed me of this victory. We began to talk not only about how technology could change the world but also about how we could impact this world.

Erica Johnson
SISTER

After Ken graduated and started working, he and Jen began to establish the life they wanted to be living. Being newlyweds, they were navigating what that was going to look like with respect to their individual families.

Ken got his first job and was learning his industry and advancing quickly. Almost before I noticed it, Ken was making good money, enjoying the benefits of a high-paying job, and living what he thought was the dream.

My brother and I had a tradition for how we spent Christmas Eve, a tradition we carried into his first year of marriage. We would sleep in the same room so we could wake up together on Christmas Day and see what Santa brought. It was so much fun growing up, but the last year we did it was different. Maybe it was different because we were older and Ken was married and starting out on his own adventure with Jen, but I missed how things used to be.

Maybe, as his sister, I tended to be more critical of him, and perhaps that isn't fair. It had nothing to do with Jen, a woman whom I had grown to love as my own sister, and it wasn't the reality of their new marriage, which can certainly change a person. He was just different.

Things really started to bother me when he and Jen started having kids. They would break their toys and Ken would just buy new ones. "Toys were meant to be broken," he would say. As a mother often living paycheck to paycheck, that was so frustrating to me. He had a nice house, nice cars, and all the other trappings of the "good life," but he didn't seem to actually place value on them, only on the status they represented.

It made me think back to the time we were little and he stole money from the church. He claimed to be using that money to help people, but the reality was that money had a hold on him in a way not uncommon today. My frustration caused a fair amount of tension between my brother and me. Perhaps I was a little jealous of the money he had compared to me; I would have loved to provide for my children the way

Ken could for his, but the attitude with which he engaged his money was maddening.

There came a point in Ken's life, however, where he radically changed his priorities. He started taking classes on financial stewardship, reoriented his life to follow a call to missions, and adopted a debt-free mindset. He passed that lifestyle and attitude on to his children and helped them understand the value of a dollar. I went from being frustrated with Ken to admiring the passion with which he approached this change.

My brother had faults. He was not a perfect person. But Ken was the first to acknowledge those areas of weakness. While he was a stubborn man, he was never so stubborn as to refuse change that needed to happen. He walked that line with grace, and sought to use those faults for good purposes, to realign them with his beliefs.

For example, I always found my brother to be a manipulative person, certainly not a flattering adjective. When we were little, he could talk his way out of anything. When he was a new dad, he would guilt people into watching his kids so he could play golf or do something else of the same sort. "Don't you want to spend quality time with your nieces and nephews?" Maybe he wasn't conscious of what he was doing, but he had a way of approaching people and manipulating them into doing what he wanted. Over time, Ken started using that skill for good. He moved from manipulating people to convincing them, a nuance that I think is very important.

Ken saw potential in others, and he "manipulated" them into seeing it, too. He became a developer, seeking to bring the best in those around him to the table. It was a skill he always had, but one he had been using the wrong way most of his life. As his younger sister, I found it inspiring to see Ken using the positive trajectory of his life to help others and move others in a similar positive direction. I became very proud of the kind of man Ken was constantly seeking to be, and I loved seeing how that positive growth continued to affect his life and the life of his family.

I miss my brother. I know this might not be the appropriate place in the story to say that, but it's true. I love him and miss him often. I didn't start my adulthood respecting or admiring Ken, but I grew to do so. The way he developed and changed continues to inspire me to live my life for Christ. I am sure you have heard enough by now about my brother's faith, and maybe you're over it. But the reality is that he was a Christian, first and foremost. If you came away from meeting my brother, it was likely the single thing you would know if nothing else. We fought a lot, and I lived a lot of my life in his shadow, but he was a good man, a genuinely loving man, and I didn't want that to go unsaid.

Dave
FATHER

In August 1998, Ken was appointed executive director of the Technologies Research Corporation in Ann Arbor, a for-profit subsidiary of the NCMS. In this position, he directed joint-venture research and development programs, primarily in the automotive and aerospace sectors. During the summer of 1999, Ken met Chad Lehner, who would become like a brother to him.

Chad Lehner
FAMILY FRIEND AND COLLEAGUE

At the intersection of Jackson and Baker Roads in Ann Arbor, there is a fairly non-descript, large white-and-green sign that lists several of the businesses lining Jackson Road. The sign is faded and somewhat obscured by some fairly tall weeds out in front.

Near the end of 2013, I happened to be driving by this sign with a co-worker. He casually pointed to the sign and said, "That has to be one of the most worthless signs on the road; I can't imagine anyone ever paying any attention to it." I laughed for a second, but as I thought about what he had said, I realized that, if it weren't for that sign, he and I wouldn't have been in the car together at that moment, nor would we likely be working for the same company. It was that non-descript sign that launched a chain of events that completely changed my life.

It was the summer of 1999, and I was fresh out of college with a master's degree in engineering. I was renting a small apartment from my girlfriend's mother so I could save money to buy a house.

I distinctly remember seeing a small advertisement on the road sign for Honey Creek Church of the Nazarene. Having been raised in a Nazarene Church, I thought I would attend and see if I liked it. My first

Sunday was sometime in July; I remember everyone being very warm and welcoming.

When I was introduced to Dave, Jerri, and Erica Johnson and they found out I was an engineer, their immediate reaction was, "You have to meet Ken!" Unfortunately, he wasn't there that day.

Little did I know I was soon to meet someone who would become one of my best friends.

A week later, I met Ken, his wife, Jen, and their children, Sydney and Erick. After church, we were all invited over to the pastor's house for dinner. Sydney was barely talking, but I fed Erick a bottle. I remember there was good food, great conversation, and card games. More importantly, though, it was the day one of the most special friendships I have ever had begun.

The impact Ken had on my life is huge. I doubt I would be married to my wife if it weren't for Ken; I certainly wouldn't have left General Motors and launched a successful career in small business if it weren't for Ken.

Our friendship wasn't coincidental, nor was it casual; it was intentional and life-- changing. I believe God has a plan for each of us. For some, it is crystal clear; others have to go digging for it.

When we met, Ken was a mid-level project manager for a small firm in Ann Arbor, made good income, had a nice car, a nice house, two kids, and a lovely wife. Being the creative guy he was, he also had a side business with some sort of 3D projection system that made hologram-like images on a TV screen. Ken was living the American dream, had a lifestyle most people could only hope to aspire to, and, if he never did anything different, would have been considered a success. It's strange, though, how God's plan may not have anything to do with either where we are in life or with our ambitions.

At Christmas in 2002, I took an impromptu trip to Florida with the Johnsons, now a four-child family.

We ate dinner after the Christmas Eve service at church. They were on their way to spend a week in Naples. They were talking about the trip and Ken suddenly said, "Hey! You should come with us!" We piled in the car around 9:00 on Christmas night and drove straight through. One of my fondest memories of Ken is listening to him sing along to Stryper songs we were blasting on the stereo, trying to do his best Michael-Sweet impression, but Ken sang bass and Sweet sings falsetto.

Funny incidents aside, I think it was on the way back from Naples the story of Ken's transformation really started. It was late at night; in fact, it was the same night Ohio State University won the national football championship title. I remember because the roads in Cincinnati were quiet, and driving through Columbus, we only saw a single car on the road. Ken got a call from an acquaintance at Delphi, an automotive technologies firm. It was an odd time for a phone call, but it was one of those moments when life suddenly takes a detour. Ken hadn't applied there and had no plan to leave his job at NCMS, but Delphi thought he would make a great licensing executive.

Dave
FATHER

In February 2003, Ken started at Delphi Corporation in Troy, MI, as commercialization and licensing executive. He was responsible for a full range of commercialization and licensing activities geared to leverage Delphi's vast technology portfolio of over 6,000 patents and its $1.1 billion annual research and development budget. While he was very effective at NCMS, Delphi offered a technology concept that spun off internally developed processes to outside industry sectors that were not necessarily automotive businesses.

It was also around this time that Ken shared with David Tait his desire to work in the mission field full-time while supporting and educating his family.

David Tait
FAMILY FRIEND AND COLLEAGUE

At Delphi, Ken was spinning off a software company whose product optimized a CNC machining program to reduce time and tooling. Ken asked me to run the business that was a joint venture between Delphi and Clark Hill, a Detroit-based law firm. The company, Precon, was not a large company and operated out of a small office building in Grosse Point, near Detroit.

Ken would meet me there and we would brainstorm how to move the business forward, as well as other challenges. I drew strength from his calm approach and the innovative ideas he presented with such passion. It was also during Ken's time at Delphi he discovered a solid state welding process called Deformation Resistance Welding (DRW) for building military vehicle space frames in a higher quality and faster process path, for which he owns patents.

Managing intellectual property and looking for small businesses with which to partner were among Ken's responsibilities at Delphi. This was when he met Rick Fortson, at the time president of Cubic Systems, Inc., a small technology company that engineered custom test equipment for the auto industry based in Ann Arbor.

Rick Fortson
FRIEND AND COLLEAGUE

My first meeting with Ken was in a little building off of a dirt road on the far west side of Ann Arbor that housed the engineering firm where I worked. We had a pond out front filled with fish, a barbecue grill out back, beer in the refrigerator, and a too-small working environment filled with clutter, computers, and equipment.

Hosting any business meeting at our office was fraught with potential difficulties stemming from the casual nature of our working environment to the logistic issues raised from the lack of space in which to hold a meeting. Every table was filled with clutter, engineering manuals, schematic diagrams, and half-finished projects. Whenever possible, we would try to hold meetings off-site to give us a chance to look more professional. My first meeting with Ken was not to be stage-managed in that fashion.

He wandered into my office unannounced; having discovered us by word of mouth, he felt he could leverage our experience in vehicle testing using custom electronics. When he showed up that morning, we were in the middle of an engineering project that had been underway for several months and for which we had been putting in long hours. The place was a mess, and we were not dressed for an important business meeting.

My business partner was a little annoyed at the interruption, but we both wanted to be as hospitable as possible. The contract engineering world lurches from feast to famine, and no opportunity to find business should go unheeded, but here was an impeccably dressed corporate executive in our midst who was clearly on a mission of his own.

Ken sat down, laughed at our awkward embarrassment about the messy, unimpressive surroundings, and said: "I can see you guys actually get to do real work here."

I vividly remember Ken's easy demeanor, engaging personality, and exuberance the day we met, trying to convince us the Federal Government really did like to fund small companies such as ours for "important" projects. Specifically, he wanted us to contribute to a military project for which there were no "off-the-shelf" products available, but for which there was a ready pool of experience to be found in small tech firms to create and integrate such equipment. It was an opportunity to work together on projects for the United States Marine Corps' Light Armored Vehicle (LAV) program.

Delphi was a member of the NCMS and had jointly developed a proposal for designing and implementing advanced sensor technologies for use in upgrading the LAV. In addition to contributions made by the institutions and companies on the team, the project was to be co-funded using grants from the Federal Government.

I was astounded when he described how long it took to prototype new devices at Delphi compared to what we could do at Cubic. The production volumes for devices like networked vehicle body modules were so high that it was impossible for Delphi to tweak a design for a low-volume production run for smaller fleet projects like the LAV project.

For example, the Light Armored Vehicle used a 24-Volt electrical system, and the Delphi module he wanted to use for vehicle data acquisition would only run at 12 Volts. Ken knew that smaller companies like Cubic could "tweak" one of their own designs to operate at various system Voltages in a time span of weeks as opposed to years, and such a modification could be performed at far lower cost than would be possible at a behemoth like Delphi. This simple chance of doing business in the automotive world was the foot in the door that would let us participate in and compete for projects with much larger corporations.

My company was comprised of a handful of Ann Arbor engineers and entrepreneurs. Shortly before that time, we transitioned from a focus on contract engineering to developing and marketing customizable hardware and software tools that could be applied to a wide variety of problems. Ken recognized our offerings could be modified to suit his project, in essence ruling out having to re-invent the wheel.

I remember being nonplussed at the time, skeptical that a diverse mix of business cultures could function together and produce anything of value. There had always been tension between large and small company culture in my experience; sometimes it produced good results, other times not so much. One reason my little firm enjoyed the respect and continued business dealings with large enterprises was a recognition that we were nimble and able to perform in ways not otherwise possible with engineers weighed down by overbearing management and pedantic corporate routine.

Ken was undeterred. He had an endless reservoir of confidence and the ability to persuade folks who were skeptical of doing things in a new way. His talent at communicating exactly what his audience needed to hear to convince them of the merits of his position in any situation was astounding. Ken's point was that every member of a large team would be able to work together effectively if they had confidence in the ability of the other team members and could see tangible results flowing from the new organization.

His enthusiasm was infectious. Ken convinced me this would be the perfect opportunity for my little company to break free from the limitations brought by being small and undercapitalized.

It was a blessing to have had Ken seek me out and show me how I could play profitably in this new world of business. At the time, our little company did not have the first clue about how to market ourselves and our services to large government-funded projects such as the one Ken brought to our door. Such opportunities are rare and can make or break a little company.

As part of shepherding me through the intricacies and politics inherent in such undertakings, Ken did his best to point out all the common ways that such relationships could fall apart. Even moving forward with modest success required careful attention to "nuts and bolts" details of billing, payment, Intellectual Property ownership and licensing, documentation and travel. The LAV Project was being coordinated by NCMS, where Ken worked prior to joining Delphi. He knew all the ins and outs for me to be able to navigate these strange new waters.

He had us immediately take advantage of membership in NCMS, which was a requirement for project membership. Ken personally vouched for Cubic with the folks at NCMS and with the other project partners, and even showed off one of the devices he had borrowed from us for that purpose. Without Ken's personal involvement, we would not have been able to independently figure out all of what we would need to know to do business with the other participants. Ken himself took ownership of the relationship with Cubic Systems, and would advocate on our part to help us get over the inevitable "speed bumps" that came up in such a large undertaking for a small company.

In particular, Ken was very anxious that we take steps to "protect" ourselves from some of the antics larger companies undertake when competing for positions with each other. Most of the companies on the LAV project were fierce competitors in the private sector as well as on other projects, where they were in direct competition for government projects, programs, and funding. Although the NCMS does a masterful job at coordinating the efforts of corporate and educational entities while working on a common project, they cannot be responsible for relationships and competitive forces that exist outside that context.

I was astonished to learn and see for myself how poorly otherwise consummate professionals can behave when status and opportunity are on the line. Ken's sense of fair play and decency was, in many ways, the "glue" that held together a complex project staffed by folks with diverse personalities and backgrounds. I have been to many large meetings that could have easily turned ugly where Ken was able to articulate competing points of view in a way that led everyone to at least agree their position was accurately portrayed. It is an amazing thing to see grown men behaving like children and to have someone step in forcefully, yet fairly, to set things back on course. Ken was masterful at defusing tension and effectively steering a gathering.

Large companies have resources and capabilities beyond the reach of small start-ups like the one for which I worked. Ken was particularly good at helping small companies avoid common pitfalls dealing with larger entities, and to work behind the scenes to grease the skids for issues like purchase orders and payment. He could also convince people of the value a small company could bring to the table. Many large companies simply do not trust a small company will be around long enough to commit to a multi-year project. This is one reason the federal government will condition grant money for proposals to projects that require participation in small businesses. Without such requirements, a larger firm might never support such a venture.

Ken was willing to put his reputation on the line in support of a smaller company's involvement with a particular project. He was equally willing to turn down the opportunity to work with a company if he felt there could be problems later on—regardless of its size or political clout. He would also not hesitate to call any company out for non-performance.

I wound up partnering with Ken in many business ventures, and over that time, I was exposed to a vast range of situations and experiences that simply would not have been possible without him.

After starting work on the LAV Project while at Cubic Systems, I left the little company I had co-founded and was hired on at Ken's new home company, Solidica, for what would be the most exciting and rewarding professional experience of my life. I met many new people, made lifelong friends, invented and fielded many new products, won multiple industry awards, and furthered my understanding of my own abilities as an effective catalyst for positive change in society through my association with Ken.

Ken planted the seeds that would alter my career arc with the initial project he had convinced me to join. He had the ability to see beyond limitations and recognize the nugget of value in a person, organization, or situation others might miss.

Chad Lehner
FAMILY FRIEND AND COLLEAGUE

In March 2003, a fiery preacher by the name of Elaine Pettit came to our church for a few nights. Her message was simple and to the point: As Christians we are to prayerfully seek God's will in our lives and constantly strive to become like Him while sharing this message with the world. Her message impacted a lot of people; many in the congregation wanted to end their careers to become ministers or serve God in other capacities.

Ken surprised me when he told me he felt the call to teach at ONU and be a missionary in Africa. Jenny felt the same. I must admit, my first thought was kind of selfish. My father told me he prayed for me to find good Christian friends who would help me on my walk. Ken and Jen had become these friends and I didn't want to lose them. They mentored me, prayed with me, and shared with me. Ken was my Sunday school teacher and my closest confidant. I loved their kids like they were family; I didn't want the Johnsons to move away.

God's plan is so cool, though; not only was I able to get closer to the Johnsons in this time, but I was also able to see, as I had never witnessed, one of the most resolute examples of God laying out His plan for someone.

When Ken got the call to become a missionary and teach, there were a few worldly obstacles in his way. First, to teach at the university level, you needed a PhD. Second, to be a missionary, you needed to have a small debt load. At the time Ken didn't have a doctoral degree and his debt load was over one- half a million dollars.

I came to terms with the fact that Ken was on a different path and eventually my friends would be moving away, but with the obstacles to overcome, I knew it was not about to be an immediate loss. My comfort in coming to terms with this concept was aided by the conviction that I was to encourage Ken and help him stay on this path. The first step came quickly.

Only a year or so after taking the job at Delphi, Ken was ready to quit. Apparently someone had taken offense to Ken discussing religion with a co-worker while riding in a car and wrote him up for it. I remember telling Ken that it was probably because he wasn't supposed to be there, he was supposed to be living in the bush somewhere in Africa, but of course that wasn't the case.

Just a few weeks after this whole ordeal, a call came in from a lady who had started a small technology firm that specialized in a new technology that used sound waves to weld layers of metal together. The name of this venture was Solidica, and she desperately wanted to grow the business and wanted to hire Ken as a marketing manager. The job was risky, the benefits not so great, and from the outside it seemed to be more risk than reward. I was still on the idea he should be witnessing to goat herders in the fields of Kenya, so I thought it was a bit crazy, but God was opening doors in a big way for the Johnsons.

Dave
FATHER

In September 2004, Ken started working at Solidica, Inc., a second-stage technology company backed by Michigan-based venture capital focused on additive manufacturing, advanced materials and vehicle-based telematics for the automotive and heavy truck industries. He was appointed as vice-president of strategic development and was responsible for international business development and marketing activities while overseeing product development and research road mapping. In 2006, Ken became president and CEO at Solidica, leading the company to expand into a variety of markets including military, distribution, aerospace, utilities, mining, and airport ground support.

Chad Lehner
FAMILY FRIEND AND COLLEAGUE

Solidica was basically a playground for materials engineers, something Ken admitted he knew nothing about. His background was in manufacturing engineering, which is about as far removed from materials as biology is from calculus. However, being the creative dealmaker that he was, Ken brokered the deal of a lifetime.

To "learn the business," he would need to be well versed in the technology of sonic welding and so Ken worked out a deal where he would be able to work full-time at Solidica and get his PhD through the Loughborough University in England. He utilized the research facilities at the Wolfson School of Engineering and the Materials Department at Loughborough in completing the requirements for the Doctor of Philosophy degree. When he had defended his dissertation successfully he called his dad and said: "Hello Dr. Johnson. This is Dr. Johnson" in typical Ken style. Dave flew to England to spend a few days with Ken and attend his graduation ceremony.

The program would only require that he travel once a quarter for research purposes, and he would be done in three years. Having spent two–and–a–half years getting a master's as a full-time student, I was decently envious.

So Ken had a new job and was on track to get his PhD. This left just one obstacle: debt. Ken sold his house and started renting. He sold the Corvette, his old Porsche, his motorcycle, his four-wheeler, and some of his furniture. I bought everything except the Corvette. The Johnsons adopted the Dave Ramsey financial principles and in just a few years were able to get their debt under control.

Early in 2007, Ken met with a group of former Marines who were basically operating as mercenaries. They had just seen the new Batman movie and wanted to build a "Bat mobile" they could use for VIP transport in high-risk areas in the Middle East.

Ken was always finding crazy opportunities, but this one stands out because it was the reason I left my comfy career at GM. I was a car guy with a lot of vehicle knowledge and Ken lured me away from GM by involving me on the ground level of a new company called GraviKor which we started in his office.

Ken's master plan was to have me operate as a part-time consultant for GraviKor and a full-time consultant for Solidica. I was ecstatic to be working with my best friend. I always described our working relationship like the old Looney Tunes cartoon with Sam the Sheepdog and Ralph the coyote. All day long, the coyote would try to come up with clever ways to catch the sheep and otherwise harm the sheepdog, only to have the sheepdog stop his every attempt. At the end of the day, the whistle would blow, each would punch the clock and say "good night, Sam ... good night, Ralph." Our relationship was often constructive adversarial business all day long, but off the clock we were back to our goofy selves.

Although the Bat mobile never came to fruition, GraviKor did win a multimillion dollar contract through the Department of Energy to investigate a new welding technology and its application to building safe and lightweight vehicles. Ken was masterful at finding money. The guy could squeeze cash out of just about anyone, and this was no exception.

Solidica was good to us. After a few years, Ken was the CEO and running the place. I was doing sales and was also the project manager. The experience we both gained was paramount in determining where we went next. Being CEO allowed Ken 4 weeks a year to do semi-annual mission trips to Kenya with teams from our church. There were times he pondered whether or not he had answered his call, but then we'd talk and he would get fired up about getting to the point where he was a full-time teacher and missionary.

Ken and Former Michigan Governor Jennifer Grandholm at Solidica

Ken and I ended up working together at GraviKor and Solidica for more than 5 years. During that time, there were ups and downs with the business, and toward the end, we had some especially lean periods where we only worked part-time at a reduced salary. There was always the temptation to leave, but God put it on my heart that I was supposed to stick with Ken until it was time for him to fully answer his call. Ken was easily distracted by new opportunities, and I felt my call at the time was to keep encouraging him to stay on track with his goal of being a missionary.

Early in 2012, I just happened to walk in on a conversation backstage at church where Jenny was sharing with the worship team something to the effect of, "Ken's interview at ONU had gone really well." I think the look of surprise was fairly evident on my face because her next statement was along the lines of "oh—you didn't know?"

The next day, I went into Ken's office and asked him if he had anything to share. I remember his goofy guilty grin as he told me he wasn't trying to keep it a secret, and he just hadn't had the chance to tell me yet. He had interviewed for the job of engineering department chair at ONU. Better yet, they would want him to lead mission trips with his engineering students to Africa and work with ANU to establish an engineering program.

It sounded like the perfect culmination of all of Ken's work to follow his call, but I had one more task to keep Ken on track.

He told me he also had an opportunity to work for Michigan State University starting businesses using the University's intellectual property. He was thinking at the time he would still do mission work at the church, but take on this new job. Joking a little, I stepped about five feet backwards. When he asked what I was doing, I said that I didn't want to be close when lightning struck. This was the last time that I had to remind him he was called to teach and serve in Africa and only one of those opportunities served his call.

After he took the position at ONU, he often mentioned the conversation we had that day. He said it was the day it finally gelled in his mind that he had achieved his call.

In my mind, Solidica was just a stepping-stone for both of us. I firmly believe that God allowed it to exist simply for Ken to achieve his call. Not long after Ken left, the company ran into some financial woes; most of the employees had to find other opportunities. The strange thing is that everyone who had to leave found something very quickly. I was able to find a great job as a program manager and even had a few of the Solidica folks hired onto our team.

Jen Johnson
WIFE

During the time we spent in Kenya working with Chief John and the people of Ewaso Ng'iro, Ken also formed a friendship with Leah Marangu, the Vice Chancellor of ANU. It's through this friendship, that ideas were explored about the possibility of starting an engineering department at ANU. Leah expressed a desire and suggested Ken apply for a Fulbright Scholarship to further explore this possibility. He certainly had the professional qualifications for the job, having been an engineer in many companies and pioneered different avenues within the field, and he was educationally qualified for the job, so we were excited.

Ken applied and was not immediately turned down, and we were encouraged. The process of picking the winner of this prestigious scholarship sponsored and funded by the U.S. State Department, was set up so if you did not hear that you were turned down, you were still in the running. We waited and waited and grew more and more excited with the thought we could actually be going as a whole family to Kenya for at least a year. It was the end of March and Ken was informed he was the alternate. Because we had gotten our hopes up by how long it took for them to decide, we were very disappointed. Why not? We felt almost sure that this was the direction God wanted us to go only for the door to be shut, but we were learning that God uses all circumstances for his glory.

We did not give up, however, on the call. Because God had begun working almost seven years prior to this, we were able to become almost completely debt free and ready to go if only God would give us the signal. As it turned out, we didn't have to wait too long.

We were in Florida on a family vacation when Ken received a call from the Engineering Chair, Mike Morgan, at ONU on New Year's Day. He and Ken had been friends since Ken was a student of Mike's when Ken was at ONU in the engineering program. Mike wanted to let Ken know he would be resigning as the Engineering chair at the end of the next semester and he was going to strongly suggest to the Dean that Ken should be the next chair. Needless to say, Ken was speechless. Here was an opportunity to fulfill his lifelong dream of teaching! Was this what God wanted us to be ready for? Was this the mission field? After all, it would combine two objectives high on Ken's list of desires. Could God be giving Ken the opportunity to use a single stone for two birds? As it happens, that is exactly what we had in store.

Matthew Heddle
FAMILY FRIEND AND COLLEAGUE

I have known Ken since before I even knew how to walk. I have worked with him at two different companies (Ann Arbor Craftsman and NCMS), played basketball with him, golfed with him, and now, though I never fully appreciated it then, there is something that seems so obvious upon reflection but was somehow lost to me among all of his other qualities.

Sure, he was at or near the top of most anybody's list of smartest people they knew. Yes, the stories of his selflessness and missionary work abound. True, his work ethic, commitment to his family, and his leadership are second to none.

After several weeks of reflection upon his life, the thing that stands out about him for me, even as a teenager, was how confident he was. He was confident in everything: his personality, his friendship, his business life, and his family life. They all seemed so easy for him. I never saw him get angry, lose control, be disrespectful, spiteful, or slanderous to another person. He had an ease and calm about him and always seemed to stand tall.

Knowing Ken for so long and having several conversations with him about his faith, I know for a fact this confidence is directly due to his relationship with Jesus Christ. Among all of his qualities, this one I admire the most. This confidence in his faith rooted through his life in every aspect. In everything he did, you could imagine God's hand on his shoulder, comforting, strengthening, and guiding him.

8
Life at Olivet

Christian engineers have tremendous potential to transform the world for Christ. Whether they go on to work for Boeing, Caterpillar, serve on the mission field or wherever, our students can be a powerful force for achieving Christ's mandate to help those in need and spread the hope of the Gospel around the world.

Dave
FATHER

Ken started working at ONU in Bourbonnais, IL in June 2012. As professor and chair of the ONU Engineering Program with concentrations in mechanical, electrical, computer, and geological engineering, he was responsible for strategic planning but also served as the leader of the ONU Advanced Additive Manufacturing Laboratory. This program involves collaboration with industry and other universities and research institutions on the advancement of disruptive additive manufacturing methods and solutions. He also continued to conduct funded research while at ONU.

Not long after becoming Chair of ONU's Department of Engineering, Ken contacted his former ONU classmate, Steven Angus, about an idea. He asked him if he would help mentor ONU engineering students interested in the automotive industry. Steve instantly said, "Yes" and started receiving emails from ONU juniors and seniors about a month later.

As of March 2014, four 2013 ONU engineering graduates were working alongside Steve at Ford Motor Company in Dearborn, Mich. Three of them were working on top–secret future model programs. Steve has received numerous comments from their supervisors, such as "Where did you find these guys? They are awesome!"

These are the kind of engineers that ONU produces.

"By the world's standards, I had achieved success in every sense of the word," Ken said in an interview shortly after joining ONU's faculty, "but I knew in my heart there had to be more. I want to help unlock the potential of technology, engineering, and innovation for a greater, Christian purpose."

Under Ken's leadership, ONU's engineering department experienced an unparalleled spike in student enrolment. He led the department through an intensive review for accreditation with the Engineering Commission for ABET, ensuring that ONU's engineering program met or exceeded all the standards for full accreditation until the next comprehensive review.

ONU's ABET accredited engineering program entered a new era with the dedication of the Martin D. "Skip" Walker School of Engineering on October 6, 2015.

Ken taught his students that their gifts and talents could be leveraged for a greater purpose, often referring to them as "missioneers." To this end, Ken led multiple engineering service projects, including taking a team of students to Swaziland in May of 2013, where they installed a water irrigation system they designed to help improve crop production and provide food to a community ravaged by HIV/AIDS.

He was also excited about a project he and his students were working on together, making use of a new lightweight metal alloy for missionary bicycles in world areas where transportation is difficult. As project manager, he led ONU's work in additive manufacturing and 3D printing projects with Nexus LCM, a leading developer of advanced 3D printing solutions.

Dr. John C. Bowling
PRESIDENT, OLIVET NAZARENE UNIVERSITY

I first encountered Ken Johnson during his undergraduate days at ONU but did not get to really know and appreciate him until he joined the ONU faculty some years later. Throughout his life, Ken was a catalytic individual. When he joined a group, took a job, or simply entered a room, the chemistry was changed.

People could tell, almost right away, Ken was a leader. He led not so much with words, though he was quite articulate; his leadership was one of example and initiative. His primary leadership currency was not authority but influence. Ken loved people and people could tell that. He was highly regarded by his peers, faculty, colleagues and was loved by his students. He had the spiritual gift of encouragement.

Ken also had the unusual characteristic of being passionate about *everything*. I am passionate about some things, but he went all out in response to whatever it was that captured his attention. He lived a big life—he worked hard, loved his family deeply and invested himself in others. As a result, Ken succeeded in every job he took, whether he was completing his education, building his own company, developing missions work, or re-engineering the ONU engineering program. He made a difference in whatever he was involved.

Houston Thompson
DEAN, SCHOOL OF PROFESSIONAL STUDIES

My first encounter with Ken was in a formal meeting at the beginning of the academic year 2012. One by one, we introduced ourselves. It was obvious from Ken's introduction he was at ONU for a reason. He wanted to honor God by investing his life in students. As Ken shared his vision for engineering at ONU, he wove it through a contextual framework of missions. For Ken, there was a direct relationship between being an engineer and being engaged in missions.

Over the course of the year, I watched and listened as Ken worked to bring his vision to fruition. He was planning, organizing, and working to build a quality engineering program and connecting it to a global focus of reaching people for Christ. In Ken's mind, the two were inseparable.

He is given credit at ONU for popularizing the term "missioneering." As Ken's Dean, I met with him at the beginning of his second academic year, in August 2013, to learn more about the engineering department and how I could better serve him and the department. We talked about academics, resources, new construction, and missions. Ken was dedicated to using his life to invest in others. He saw the heart and possibilities of others and invested himself in trying to help them grow and become all they could be in Christ. Ken saw things in others that he would latch onto and nurture to help them grow and mature.

As Ken worked on leading construction for the new engineering wing, he always thought about ways he could make it the best it could be for faculty and students. He would plan and scheme to surprise faculty with something new or something they were not expecting. He was continuously thinking of ways he could make it special.

Doug Perry
VICE PRESIDENT FOR FINANCE

When Ken arrived, the department of engineering took off like a rocket. We increased our majors exponentially. Students were really drawn to Ken, and he mentored and motivated them, not only for engineering but also for Kingdom service. They took a trip to Swaziland to work on humanitarian projects. Every time I heard Ken speak, I was so proud he was an Olivetian and an academic leader at ONU.

I remember one time when he spoke to our Board of Trustees and we were all so moved by his testimony and his work with the students at ONU. It was a real missional moment. Because of the growth in the number of engineering students under Ken's leadership, we realized we would need to add facilities and faculty to the department. Ken and I began working on a plan with our architects to add an addition to Reed Hall of Science for an engineering wing, which opened in the fall of 2014, the year following his passing. Nearly all the design of the new facility was directed and planned by Ken. It was also designed to partner with private and government industry in research and development projects. Our students work with various companies on research projects and gain very practical experience in the field of engineering.

Dr. Dennis Crocker
VICE PRESIDENT FOR ACADEMIC AFFAIRS

In the conversations, emails, and phone calls, I sensed his energy and his enthusiasm. He had this kind of boundless eagerness for everything he did which was contagious and which was sensed by everyone he met. He was *all in* whatever he did. Nothing he did was half– hearted. He showed us and demonstrated what being a fully committed Christian looked like, and he did it in such an engaging and attractive way that we all wanted to be like him.

To say that Ken has had an impact on the engineering program at ONU is extremely understated. He believed, and we now see more clearly, that engineering is missional. It is not just preparing students for good–paying jobs--it is as Ken said *"missioneering"*.

Dr. Bowling has said that Ken was a catalyst, and I think that this term describes Ken's life beautifully. A *catalyst* is said to be a substance that increases the rate of a chemical reaction of two or more reactants. This is what Ken did!

Ken has had a profound influence on my life. He has made me a better person and a better administrator; he has challenged me to improve and to refine my vision and way of leading. My view of academic administration involves aspects of missions, excellence, and entrepreneurial creativity. It is Ken's influence that helped me think through and develop the component of entrepreneurial creativity. He challenged me to think outside the box and to ask what's best for our students in different, more effective ways.

His *all out* commitment to everything he did has inspired and challenged me and all of us to do the same. Essentially, as the Apostle Paul said, to do everything, in word or deed, to the glory of God. We will never be the same because of Ken Johnson!

John Mongerson
EXECUTIVE DIRECTOR OF DEVELOPMENT AND FOUNDATION

I have shared with numerous people a description of Ken. It developed from something a colleague said to describe him. I have shared with many that, in our view, if one could construct an ideal college professor, they would be essentially what we had in Dr. Ken Johnson.

I remember Ken when he was at ONU, but actually knew and worked with him a relatively brief time. My short time with Ken left me with several outstanding memories.

Ken was a genuine friend to me. Most friendships of this strength and comfort seem to require far more time to build. Not so my friendship with Ken. Further, I perceived it was similar with others. Ken was truly remarkable and unusual in this respect, being able to develop profound and meaningful relationships quickly and easily, regardless of disparate backgrounds or dissimilar life experiences.

It blew my mind how Ken was always so accomplished, yet so willing to lend a hand. I often wondered how someone with such tremendous responsibilities at ONU could remain so willing to speak at a church or campus event, meet with prospective students, and work like a development officer with our donors. He was incredible! Ken would always respond in the affirmative when we hesitatingly inquired if he might help with some project or event. Maybe it was exploitative asking an already busy person for help when we knew he wouldn't say no, but I think not. Ken's unique skill set equipped him best to serve myriad needs. We asked him not for the guaranteed yes, but for the enthusiastic passion with which he alone would tackle the project. He was a one-of-a-kind individual.

Dr. Glen Rewerts
CHAIR, DEPARTMENT OF BUSINESS

It was sometime in the early spring of 2013, the snow had long been gone, the neighborhood had been washed clean with a couple of good thunderstorms, and everything was bright, sunny, and perfect for an Airsoft battle. My son, Cully, was celebrating his twelfth birthday. It was, perhaps, his last time as an Airsoft soldier. He celebrated along with thirteen other soldier buddies from school and around the neighborhood. Calls were made, hot dogs and buns were ready with condiments, and we had extra ketchup for fake blood. Everything was in place for the big party battle.

The day before the event, Tara, my wife, and our three kids were in town running last minute errands when my arm began shaking, and I started feeling a striking pain run up my chest. Normally, I ignore most common sense signs like that and keep driving. This time, however, Tara convinced me to turn into St. Mary's emergency room to get checked out. To make a long story short, I was stuck in the hospital overnight for observations with the choice of rescheduling Cully's party to another day or scrambling to find a friend to be the captain of his motley crew of preteen boys crawling, through the brush, dirt, and briars in our make-shift battlefield.

As I started making the calls, too many of my friends knew what was involved, too many had heard the stories of injury and of ketchup. None of them were brave enough.

Jeff Enfield, a long-time soccer friend, stepped up, but I instinctively knew it would take at least two rookies to fill the shoes of this veteran. Ken was just an acquaintance; I had known him briefly at work as we both served on the same committee as Chairs of our respective departments. He was always suited with a tie, trimmed and groomed. Everybody knew Ken as a highly talented, energetic visionary who was sacrificing a promising career in the engineering field for the cause of Christ in the form of advancing ONU. But could he lead 14 unknown pre-teens with full army gear in an Airsoft war on an unfamiliar battlefield on behalf of someone he barely knew? I knew him to have quite the full schedule, his own wife and children, a new job, a position that could be all-consuming, and a growing reputation for diving in and pouring himself into the engineering department. I could only guess his schedule was too tight to mess with something like this. Besides, he barely knew me.

Without other options, I called Ken, and I remember his response as if it were yesterday. "Sure I can do that, it sounds fun. Don't worry about a thing, just get better." While I gleefully reveled in the fruits of his ignorance, the Spirit corrected me and asked, "Would you step up and help an almost stranger, like Ken Johnson just did?" I felt the first impact of Ken Johnson's life upon my own.

When I came home from the hospital, it happened to be at the exact time the captain and his troops were marching back from the battlefield. They were covered in dirt and the boys started telling their war stories. One of the stories that came out from the troops was how they got chased from the battlefield—five acres of scrub brush—by the lot's owner. I didn't know who owned it, but Ken got to find out. It turned out the owner had been passing through the neighborhood, saw the boys, and informed them they were trespassing. So there Ken Johnson stood, doing a favor for someone he barely knew, hot, sweaty, dirty, with mostly unknown camouflaged kids, stuck in the middle of the street. They had already had a great time, but he never brought the issue up, the boys did. When I apologized for the situation, he simply said, "Oh, it was fun. Thanks for asking me. We had a great time." I don't think I've met a more selfless person to this day than Ken proved to be after having met me merely weeks before.

Chad Lehner
FAMILY FRIEND AND COLLEAGUE

After Ken and Jen moved to Illinois, I wasn't sad as I had originally thought I would be. I actually felt closer to Ken than I had in years. I didn't miss him because we still talked regularly; in fact, we even started a joint venture between ONU and my new company. Every time I saw Ken, he would tell me that he had never been happier.

The last time I saw Ken was less than 2 weeks before he passed. The family was up for a Sunday visit, and we went out to dinner after church with our mutual friends, the Lamberts. There was a glow about that afternoon; Ken was so pumped about the current mission project that his students were working on. They were designing a pumping station to bring fresh water to a village in Kenya where the kids couldn't go to school because they spent their day walking 7 miles one way to fetch water. They were also working on an "ultimate missions vehicle," using the old H2 Hummer that we had modified for the GraviKor project. The idea was that it would be a modular vehicle that could be quickly changed from an ambulance to a water pumping station to a people hauler to suit the needs of the team using it.

Ken had promoted the term "missioneering" for the projects, but it is also a perfect word to summarize God's plan for him. During dinner, he gave me a "missioneering" t-shirt and told us he wanted everyone on his team or supporting his program to have one. Our dinner conversation that day lasted all the way into the parking lot. There were lots of hugs and when my wife and I got into the car, we commented on how wonderful the time was.

Taylor Westrate
CLASS OF 2014

A memory I have of Dr. Johnson took place in Technical Communication class. We were practicing giving updates on our topics. I stood up and got completely held up on a word; I just couldn't spit it out. It was the first time that that had ever happened to me, so I laughed about it after I finished and just brushed it off. Later, Dr. Johnson was giving feedback on each person's description.

He said, "Well, we all know how Taylor messed up there, but what he did very well was that he laughed it off. He didn't get hung up on it, and sometimes you mess up and it can ruin your day. He just laughed it off, and showed his cute Taylor smile." I could not believe he said that; I have never been so embarrassed in a class, but it was hilarious. To this day, every time I smile around my fellow engineers they say, "Aw, look at that cute Taylor smile." It is crazy how the little things stay with you.

Dr. Johnson was an immensely intelligent man, but he still was able to come down to your level to explain things without sounding condescending; he seemed like an average guy whenever you talked to him. He was extremely personable and never had a bad attitude toward anyone. He could see the light in everything and could make the best out of any circumstance.

I don't feel a huge calling toward missions, but his sacrificial heart makes me consider it. He was willing to give up so much just to do the right thing. Even coming to ONU's campus was a huge sacrifice for him. I'm sure he could have gone to work for about any company out there or be on the faculty at any university, making twice the amount he made at ONU, but he didn't. He wanted to expand their engineering program and leave his mark on his alma mater. If I can die half the person he was, I will be overjoyed.

Jesse Erickson
CLASS OF 2014

Ken Johnson was a mentor, the greatest mentor for which I could have hoped. I could walk into his office at any given time, and he would drop anything he was doing to talk to me for however long I needed. He was a very generous man in this way. He gave his time, attention, energy, and heart to students and colleagues every day.

I only knew Dr. Johnson for 1 year and 4 months. In that very little stretch of time, he changed my life. He helped rocket ONU's engineering department to new heights and brought new ideas and new direction to the school and its students. Instead of talking about his vision, he went out and made it a reality. He had his focus on the One who makes all change happen and submitted his work to the Creator. He knew he was only an instrument in the hands of the Father.

Christians talk about allowing their lives to reflect God, but Ken practiced what he preached. It makes me so sad to know a man as young as Ken was only given 43 years to live. I don't understand why it upsets me so much except that, for being such a shining example of Christ, I believe he had more to give. He impacted me to the point of missing him on a continual basis, even all this time after his passing.

Ken's life highlighted the idea of "who I am" versus "who I want to be." Ken, while being content with what God placed before him, never allowed complacency to get in the way of growth and change. He sought new and challenging opportunities to better himself, and I appreciate that example as much as anything about Ken. He encouraged me to never stop learning, always put God first, and to go and do likewise (as Jesus encouraged his disciples after washing their feet).

To this day, I find it odd that a man who I knew so briefly could have such power over the person I am and the goals I've set for my life, but it's encouraging to know that a short window of time can make such a difference. It gives perspective on the gift of life each of us is given.

Yonda Abogunrin
CLASS OF 2014

One of my favorite courses with Dr. Johnson was Technical Communication. Dr. Johnson was passionate and energetic in teaching this course because he knew that having very good technical communication skills will enhance our careers as professional engineers. Much like our other engineering classes, Dr. Johnson focused on the technical materials in his classes. He taught his students how to approach and solve engineering problems. However, in all the courses I took with Dr. Johnson, I was impressed with his utmost emphasis on leadership qualities.

Dr. Johnson had a different vision for his students as engineers. He didn't envision his students working as engineers, sitting behind desks and crunching out numbers. No. He had a higher expectation and vision for his students. He taught us to be technically sound as engineers, but, more importantly, he envisioned us as engineers who would stand out as leaders, engineers who would use their technical knowledge and venture into leadership roles. This vision he had guided the way he taught his classes. To me, this quality not only made him a good teacher, but it also enabled me to start thinking on a bigger scale of what I would like to do with my career. His vision for us was an eye-- opener for me.

Amanda Luby
CLASS OF 2013

Dr. Johnson was truly a remarkable teacher. His enthusiasm was not just for the subject material but also for teaching, in general, as was apparent from the moment he walked into the classroom. His passion for teaching at Olivet led him to steer the department toward a new building, a new direction, and a new chapter in its history.

Dr. Johnson was very open about his love for and faith in the Lord, both in and out of the classroom, and he often started class with a devotion. I remember seeing him in the hallway shortly after chapel one day, and he was so excited about the privilege of going to chapel and hearing people share about their faith.

Dr. Johnson was also remarkably generous. On two or three occasions, he bought pizza for the entire senior design class because the class met during lunch. For the senior design class, he also purchased engineering notebooks embossed with "Olivet Nazarene University Department of Engineering" in which we could keep work for our projects. I still have my notebook, and every time I look at it, I think of Dr. Johnson.

One of the most amazing characteristics of Dr. Johnson was his ability to inspire people. Although Dr. Johnson's enthusiasm in the classroom inspired my interest in the class material, it was his passion for teaching that inspired me to commit to becoming a professor of engineering. I had considered teaching for many years—in fact, at one point, prior to college, I had considered becoming an elementary school teacher. Throughout my first three years of college, several of my professors had affirmed my ability and calling to teach, but I had not really thought that my dream to teach engineering at the college level could actually become a reality.

Then Dr. Johnson arrived at ONU my senior year. Like my other professors, he recognized my calling to teach, but he took it one step further. He and I began discussing the possibility of me teaching engineering at the college level—at ONU! Dr. Johnson's confidence that I could become an engineering professor, and the fact he was seriously considering letting me teach at ONU, encouraged me to do everything I could to make it happen. As a result, I applied to the graduate program at Purdue University with the goal of obtaining my Masters in Electrical Engineering. Dr. Johnson, like the rest of the engineering professors at ONU, was willing to write a letter of recommendation for my application to Purdue: I firmly believe that the letters of recommendation they wrote for me secured the teaching assistantship that provided me with a full-ride to Purdue.

Only five days after taking my last final at Purdue, I found myself back at ONU interviewing for a full-time faculty position in ONU engineering. Four days later, on my graduation day, I received word that I was being offered a contract to teach at ONU.

I am currently in my first year of teaching at ONU, and I honestly don't believe I would be where I am today without the encouragement and guidance of Dr. Johnson.

Jared Dennis
CLASS OF 2015

Dr. Johnson was extremely knowledgeable and explained the cool, real-life applications of the concepts we were learning, but he was also very patient as he taught, leaving no question unanswered. He challenged us to learn and perform to the best of our abilities, without being too strict or overbearing. His Materials class is one of my favorite courses I took (even with struggling to stay awake at 8 a.m.), because I felt like I was truly learning from someone who not only knew the material inside and out but loved what he did and loved when students learned. On top of it all, the absolute most impressionable thing was how you could clearly see how he was living his faith in all that he did. His passion for missions overflowed and inspired me, and you could clearly tell he did everything for the glory of God.

He exemplified how to be a man of God through the profession of engineering. I want to be like him in his loving, caring nature for his family, students, and friends. His passion for missions—for being the hands and feet of God by using his talents to address the needs of others—was incredible. His faith was genuine and international, and I really hope that I can be like him in that way. Dr. Johnson was the most influential, genuine, and respected professor I had.

Hongyan (Addie) Zhang
CUSTODIAN, OLIVET NAZARENE UNIVERSITY

When I just think about what to write down for Dr. Ken Johnson, his voice and expression come to mind. It feels like he's still sitting down at the front desk to talk to me. It feels like he didn't leave us.

Over the summer I cleaned the Reed Hall of Science building, and I knew one office was for a new professor. On summer vacation, I didn't have a chance to meet him; on his desk were two big glass jars. One was candy and the other of candy bars. At that time, I thought this professor must be a fat guy. Over the summer, teenagers at College Church had a trip together for 1 week. My friend told me one engineer professor's son was friendly with my son. This boy's name was Erick Johnson.

Dr. Joe, an engineering professor, introduced me to Dr. Ken Johnson. Dr. Ken went to China a few years ago. I'm Chinese, and our children knew each other. I knew he had two boys and two girls. My son had only been in the U.S. for 1 year and I hoped he could make friends. I invited Dr. Ken's family over to my house for Chinese food. His wife is an attractive lady. We had a good time. After that, we occasionally met in the morning and always talked a little bit.

In the summer of 2013, I bought a house. But that was a difficult time for me. The bank didn't give me a loan. I had some furniture I needed to put somewhere. I met Dr. Ken at church. I told him my problem. Dr. Ken said if I needed help, I could call him, and he could let me put the furniture in his storage for two months. Finally I bought that house. Dr.

Ken came with his two boys to help me move. He also told me he could fix anything by himself. He said that if my house ever had a problem, I should ask him for help.

My son had been in the U.S. for a short time. He didn't have friends because he always played games at home. A few times Dr. Ken talked to me, hoping to find some way to help my son.

On the day Dr. Ken passed away, my friend called me to tell me the bad news. My heart was broken and my tears couldn't stop. We lost a good friend. He was such a kind, nice person. I don't know why he had to die so young. Dr. Ken lived as a Christ like example.

9
The Last Race

John Ford
FRIEND AND COLLEAGUE

In one sense, Ken's trip to the 2013 Iceman Cometh Challenge began around 5:00 a.m. on November 1, 2013. He would have left his house in Kankakee, IL around that time in order to attend a meeting in Ann Arbor at 10:00 a.m. In a very different, probably more real, sense, Ken's trip to the same race began a year earlier, at the 2012 race.

Run on the first weekend in November, the Iceman Cometh Challenge is equal parts mountain bike festival, social gathering, and cross-country-style mountain bike race. The race itself is the largest mountain bike race in the world, with over 4,000 participants. The course runs miles through the woods and fields, from Kalkaska to the outskirts of Traverse City.

Ken's final bike race

The race itself is physically demanding: 31 miles over a mix of single track trails and two track fire roads, the course was set on deep, sandy soil. Participants endured 1500 feet of hill climbs, some with grades greater than 10 %.

To give you an idea of the challenge involved, the winning time for the 2012 race was 1 hour 37 minutes. The median time was 2 hours 41 minutes, and the last rider exited the course after 6 hours 2 minutes.

A physical challenge of that type requires training and planning to avoid "bonking". Bonking is bicycle slang for what marathoners call "hitting the wall". It happens when extreme exercise depletes the glycogen stored in a body's muscles and liver, causing sudden and severe fatigue.

Ken bonked during the 2012 race.

It was probably easy for him to get lulled into a false sense of confidence because Ken was a genuinely gifted athlete. In his adult years, he competed in road races and triathlons and rode his mountain bike at the Brighton Recreation Area for fun. We are sure he assumed a bicycle ride through the Michigan woods would be a veritable walk in the park. Little did he know.

Ken's time for the 2012 race was 3 hours 18 minutes. It wasn't a bad time, but it was certainly disappointing for him personally. Shortly after he crossed the finish line, Ken was determined to return the following year better prepared to complete the challenging race.

Afterwards, Ken described the ride as "more difficult than Marine Corps basic training." And it probably was; the Marines make certain their trainees have ample nutrition and hydration, something that wasn't the case with the Iceman Cometh Challenge.

As soon as we started discussing returning for the race in 2013, Ken immediately said, "Yes! Redemption is needed." While Ken had nothing to prove to anyone other than himself, he was going to see to it he completed with a more acceptable time the next year.

* * *

On November 1, 2013, I met Ken around 9:50 a.m. in the offices of North Coast Technology Investors. Ken, Hugo Braun of North Coast, Dave Tait, and I met to discuss the marketing of Solidica's product, DuraTi. Even though Ken had left Solidica to join ONU, he was still actively helping Solidica achieve success with DuraTi.

Ken greeted me with a handshake and a big, warm smile. He was uniquely engaging. I used to be surprised how many people viewed Ken as their closest friend, but I've since come to understand and appreciate his ability to connect with people because he genuinely cared about them.

After wrapping up our discussion, Dave Tait went on his way then Hugo, Ken, and I met Tim to load bicycles for the trip north. Tim had rigged a utility trailer with bicycle fork mounts, making it perfect for moving the group's bicycles.

From there, it was a short drive to the Panera restaurant on Lee Road for a quick lunch, after which Ken and I rode together to the Braun family cottage on Higgins Lake.

The Brauns have a charming cottage that's been in their family for multiple generations, dating back to when the Michigan forests were clear cut during the 19th century. Hugo graciously invited us to stay at the cottage before and after the race.

The ride from Ann Arbor to Higgins Lake gave Ken and me about two hours of time to talk. That's when I learned, among other things, of Ken's training for the 2013 race.

One of Ken's training stories was about a combined car trip and bike ride in which Jen dropped Ken off then met him farther down the road. There was a bit of a tailwind and Ken was flying down the road, but he missed a turn and wound up riding miles in the wrong direction. Everything got sorted out eventually, and he met up with Jen, and truthfully, the extra training miles did him plenty of good.

We also spoke about family and his work at ONU. Ken took great delight in the development of his four children: physically, mentally, and spiritually. Even when the four of them and Jen were physically distant, they were never far from Ken's thoughts.

Mission trips were a prominent and recurring theme in Ken's life, both as a youth when he accompanied his parents to Africa and as an adult when he organized trips for the Nazarene Church in Brighton. Now he was doing it for ONU, where he popularized the word "missioneering" to describe the use of engineering skills in mission work. Ken was good at capturing ideas in a single word or phrase.

During our ride, Ken wondered if 2014 was the right year for Bethany to go on a mission trip to Africa. He felt previous mission trips transformed his life, and the same was true for Jen and the older children, Sydney, Erick, and Luke. He felt the same would hold true for Bethany.

After much conversation and light traffic, we arrived at Higgins Lake. From there, we carpooled with Hugo, Tim and his wife Robin, and Dan Foster to Traverse City to check in for the race and make a few last minute clothing purchases. Ken found a great deal on cycling gloves, which we both bought.

Then it was back to Higgins Lake to meet with the rest of our group— Gregg Hammerman and Paul McReadie—for dinner. A pasta salad Ken brought was the main course, supplemented by salad, fruits, and vegetables brought by other folks.

After dinner and friendly conversation, Ken retired to one of the bedrooms to read his Bible before turning in for the night. The rest of us likewise made it an early evening.

*　*　*

The following morning dawned cool and wet on Higgins Lake. It was another rainy day in a series of rainy days. I worried all the rain might leave the course slow and muddy, but that proved to be a misplaced concern. The rain actually compacted the sand and made for faster and easier bicycling.

Gregg's crockpot oatmeal was the main course at breakfast, accompanied by Paul's breakfast burritos, and coffee, toast, and fruit. The breakfast burritos were of dubious nutritional value before a bicycle race, but they sure tasted good.

We carpooled to Kalkaska for the start of the race. Four thousand racers cannot leave all at once, so each racer is assigned to a wave and the waves leave three minutes apart. Based on our times from 2012, Ken, Tim, and I started in adjacent waves. I was the first of us three to depart and rode slightly faster than Ken and Tim, so I never saw them on the course.

Both Tim and Ken were riding well, on pace to finish in around three hours, when Ken fell. Tim was the second rider to arrive and provided most of the information about Ken's care.

There's an unwritten code among bicycle riders that you stop to help fellow riders in need, which thankfully happened in Ken's case. A rider saw Ken go down, stopped to check on him, got no verbal response, checked for a pulse, and immediately began CPR.

Tim was on the trail just slightly behind them and arrived almost immediately afterward. He stopped to assist before he even realized the downed rider was Ken. Tim and the first rider continued CPR as others stopped, including a cardiac surgeon and a nurse who lived nearby. Other riders kept stopping, and those who weren't part of the CPR chain formed a prayer chain.

Because the finish line was close, an EMT unit was there within minutes and took over Ken's treatment. In spite of the immediate first aid, Ken never regained consciousness and passed away.

Tim Allen
FRIEND

I came across Ken at 2:03 p.m. Since only one person was there and I was the second to stop, I would say his collapse occurred within a minute of my arrival. I removed the bike and laid his legs straight before calling 911.

I tried calling Hugo and Robin at 2:20 p.m. when I was relieved from doing CPR, and we heard the ambulance arriving. It probably took less than 3 more minutes for them to reach us, so Ken had EMT support within 20 minutes of his fall.

They had to shock him, administer some drugs, get the automatic compression machine on him and get him on a backboard, so they probably worked on him less than 10 minutes before they transported him. I gave the police my information and Terry, a nurse who lived nearby, took the bike at 2:35 p.m., when I recorded her number in my phone.

Based on the time it took to get Ken, it should have taken around 20 minutes for Ken to arrive at the hospital, so from the time he collapsed until his arrival at the hospital, it was less than 50 minutes.

During the race, Ken, who left before me, had about an 11 minute lead on my pace. While I had picked up my pace toward the end, in order for his lead to evaporate so heavily, Ken would have had to be struggling for a time before he fell. Additionally, based on the position of Ken's bike when he fell over, he must have been travelling very slowly at the time of his collapse.

John Ford
FRIEND AND COLLEAGUE

I started a thread on the Michigan Mountain Bike Association (MMBA) forum to thank people who came to Ken's aid. With kind assistance from Tom Herman and the Fellowship of Christian Athletes, we organized a ride in Ken's memory at the Brighton Recreation Area on Saturday, May 24, 2014.

Members from Ken's family attended, along with the Fellowship of Christian Athletes, the Wheels in Motion Racing Team, Team RWB (a group dedicated to helping wounded veterans), the Nazarene Church in Brighton, and dozens of others.

Dr. Dave Johnson, Ken's father, did his first ever single track ride on his son's old bicycle. The ride was mixed with all the emotions you'd expect. We were so sad to be cycling amidst the loss of such a dear friend, but there was such joy in what we were doing. The grief was still close enough to not be far enough away, and many of us were fluctuating between the highs and lows of the occasion.

Epilogue

Dave and Jerri
FATHER AND MOTHER

And just like that, we reach the end of our son's story but only in the physical sense. Yes, our son Ken passed away in 2013, and he is no longer an active part of our lives, but to say his life is over does not fully acknowledge the legacy he left behind.

We hope you have seen through the telling of our son's life by those who knew him well just how ordinary a person he was. He struggled with many of the same personal issues plaguing people all over the world. He had doubts. He had obstacles to overcome. He wrestled with profound questions about his purpose. But in all circumstances, Ken grew to rely on his faith for strength. He didn't always know how circumstances were going to turn out, but he sought always to position himself to best serve God however God saw fit. One day he told us that he had recently discovered something about himself. He said, "I'm not normal." We wish we would've asked him what he meant by that. Two of the words in the dictionary associated with the word "normal" are "average" and "typical". We will leave it up to the readers of this book to decide what he might have intended to imply by that statement. He was a caring, loving man who gave selflessly to those in his life. He told us that if there was ever anything we needed or wanted to let him know. He invested in others and developed the God-given talents he saw in them waiting to be used for the Kingdom. We could all benefit by thinking of the acronym RUN in the following way: U (you) are the link between matching R(resources) with N(needs).

Two weeks before his death, Ken gave Dave his next to the last gift, a ticket to the Michigan vs. Indiana football game in Ann Arbor on October

19, 2013. He, Erick, Luke, and Dave went together. On November 8, Dave's birthday and Ken's funeral, Dave received his last gift, a framed picture of the four of them taken at the game by an usher. Ken had planned to give Dave this for his birthday. Even in death, Ken was a giver.

Ken, Erick, Luke, and Dave at their last football game at U of M

We miss him. We certainly miss him each day. Even though we miss him, we are reminded of him each day when we hear from those in our community how he touched their lives and how he helped them, even without knowing it, to confront the ways they were living their lives. More than anything, Ken exemplified what it means to be a good steward: he used responsibly the resources with which God entrusted him and multiplied those resources for the benefit of the one he served. We can think of no higher honor for which to remember Ken and with which to conclude the story of his short but powerful life than a sermon. In the following pages, you will read a sermon Ken gave about stewardship. It highlights the transformative changes he underwent in his young adult life as he sought to be faithful and submissive to the Lord.

Beyond the sermon, you will find different appendices comprised of sentiments from friends, family, and students of Ken's. While they didn't necessarily fit in the narrative of our son's life, we believed it was important context for you, the reader, to have and also for those who wrote it to see in tribute to Ken.

We thank you so much for being a part of our son's legacy, even if only in reading about the life he lived. We hope his story impacted you in some way and you were encouraged to live a life in service to God. Each day we are given is a gift we can use or waste, and Ken wasted as few as he could. We hope you will also use well your days and live them for the highest purposes.

-Dave and Jerri Johnson

07/08/12 Ken's last entry in his log. "Today is my 42 birthday and I cried. I didn't cry because I was sad, I cried for happiness over the gift Sydney left for me to find when I woke up. On a large piece of poster paper she wrote the 42 reasons why she loved me, and they were amazing. As a dad, there are times you're not quite sure you're making a difference or even if you're doing a good job. Sidney's gift alleviated those fears in a powerful way, It is a firm reminder to parents that your kids are watching closely, and they are looking for Godly attributes that support the way their creator made them."

Ken

Ken Johnson
A Sermon on Stewardship

July 29, 2012

For those of you who don't know me, I am Ken Johnson, the former Missions Director here at Brighton Church of the Nazarene. I say former because I was recently appointed to a new position about which I will share in a moment.

The message I want to share today is about stewardship, and I'm going to come right to the point here so as to give context for the rest of our time together: A life of good stewardship becomes a story worth telling.

Let's take a look at Psalm 78, which illustrates the importance of telling stories:

> *O my people, hear my teaching; listen to the words of my mouth. I will open my mouth in parables, I will utter hidden things, things from of old- what we have heard and known, what our fathers have told us. We will not hide them from their children; we will tell the next generation the praise-worthy deeds of the Lord, his power, and the wonders he has done. He decreed statutes for Jacob and established the law in Israel, which he commanded our forefathers to teach their children, so the next generation would know them, even the children yet to be born, and they in turn would tell their children.*

As Christians, what sort of stories are worth telling? It's the ones where lives were changed, where those in need were helped, where risk was taken in faith, and where Christ was revealed through us. Those are the stories that live beyond the ones who tell them. They are told to children, and grandchildren, to friends, and friends of friends. God provides many examples of such stories. Moses, Noah, David, and Gideon all have those stories, but others exist that are simple examples of strident faithfulness and a willingness to serve. They are the lasting stories, the ones that really happened. Tall tales are good, but those often don't pass beyond a generation, and they generally don't inspire others or change lives. And sometimes the best stories never get told because the subject is trapped in bondage.

My story was well on its way to becoming a story in that vein: untold because I was holding myself back from telling it. Let me quickly lay my story out for you to see. We will start by going back 8 years. I was what they call a "fast-tracker," a young executive well ahead of my peers and moving quickly up the ladder. I was smiling most of the way up, and I had more hair then than I do now, but I didn't realize how far I was from God and how far I was from being in a position to fulfill his call on my life.

In 2004, two colossal forces were set to collide: my poor stewardship of the resources I had been, rooted in a worldly financial ideology, and God's desire to set me on a path toward him.

That year I bought a lot of cool stuff. Cars and other toys were high on my list, including a sparkly new Corvette. But my life wasn't like those of the rich and famous. It was the lifestyle of the blind and selfish.

I don't mean to imply material possessions are in and of themselves bad. God loved King David in spite of his wealth and palatial living. He loved David because his heart was yearning toward God. In my case, these things became an entrapment because I had bought into the world's view of how to handle money. Ultimately, it left my family mired in debt, completely unable to answer God when he called.

And call he did. It was late in 2004, at the peak of my foolishness. I used to wonder why God waited until I had loaded up on stuff before he made himself fully known. I think it was because he wanted the stark contrast, and he wanted the change to be painful enough to be permanent. He placed desire in my life to submit completely to him, to seek him out and understand his ways, and to prepare to be used for whatever end he had in mind.

I didn't realize God had been planting seeds throughout my life and was now looking for a harvest. In order to bring that reality to bear, I had to undo a lifestyle that had become oppressive. First Chronicles 29:11-12 made a few things pretty clear:

Everything in the heavens and earth is yours, O Lord, and this is your kingdom. We adore you as being in control of everything. Riches and honor come from you alone, and you are the Ruler of all mankind; your hand controls power and might, and it is at your discretion that men are made great and given strength.

The question, then, becomes not about the 10 percent, or the tithe, but about the 100 percent, the entirety which we understand Biblically to belong to God. The notion of a tithe, while important, can falsely lead to the impression the other 90 percent is ours to do with what we will, when such an idea is farthest from the truth. When I began to understand stewardship as responsible use of all I had for the purposes of God, it made each penny I spent not a matter of my priorities but of God's.

The idea of buying my Corvette had been that I was using my 90% to buy it, but when a missions trip came along a short while later, I was inclined to join but was inhibited by a $770 payment each month that kept me from going.

There are 2,350 verses in the Bible on how to handle money and possessions. Jesus talked almost as much about money as any other topic. I don't think it was because He needed our money but because He knew the stumbling block it could become to having a healthy relationship with Him.

In truth, God is pleased when we demonstrate good stewardship. In the parable of the talents, we hear the words, "Well done, good and faithful servant; you were faithful with a few things; I will put you in charge of many things." And we know we cannot serve two masters, so it comes down to a choice: Will God submit to your material desires, or will it be the other way around?

Debt is not a good thing, be it financial debt, or debt of a less tangible kind. When you borrow, you owe the lender. That bond of debt keeps you from the freedom of independence. You become a slave to the one you owe. But being out of debt became a reward for obedience as we are told in the 28th chapter of Deuteronomy, "...You shall lend to many nations, but you shall not borrow."

To get out of debt, God compels us to be content, to stop borrowing, and to pray. Such a Christian life requires good discipline, commitment, and trust; it becomes a radically different lifestyle from what we are told is worth pursuing.

God, in his glory, is assessing our stewardship. A bad steward will be removed from the position to which he was entrusted, as we are told in Luke 16. It is important to note the size of the resources committed to our stewardship by God is irrelevant to our responsibility. "He who is faithful in very little is faithful also in much; and he who is unrighteous in a very little thing is unrighteous also in much." Luke 16:10

Our part in God's call to save others is our waiting story. Some have started their stories, some are in the middle, and others have told their story and passed on. How does the story play out? Are there changes we need to make in how we live to be better stewards of the story we are telling?

After 2004 came and went, Jen and I were confronted with two diametrically opposed concepts, and we sought to put God's call on our life ahead of the money and materials we had stored up for ourselves. We made radical changes to the way we lived and got ourselves out of debt so we could enter into a season of missions work.

Eventually, God brought our family to Bourbonnais, IL, where I started teaching as the chair of the engineering department at ONU. Not only am I mentoring college students at a critical time in their lives, but it includes annual summer mission trips all over the world.

As great as this opportunity is, my story is being built on the faithfulness of even greater stories that were told before. Stories of early founders of ONU who gave everything they had to start the school, not knowing it would grow from 10 students to nearly 5,000. Stories of BNC members who committed faithfully to going on mission trips to Kenya. Stories of people who continue to wrestle with the various calls God has placed on their lives.

Big stories are great, and certainly we all are a part of a few. The story God has plays out in some big ways, but more often than not, the critical moments come in the little things, the small ways we are obedient to Him. Daily being available and flexible to respond to His presence in our lives is important because Christian stewardship serves as the bedrock for our obedience.

Thank you, and may God bless you today.

Appendix A
Reflections from Family

Sydney Johnson
DAUGHTER

I recently had my first day of college at ONU. The plan was that I would be a student, and you would be teaching. We had plans to have lunch together in Ludwig (even though that's totally not cool to eat with your Dad in public) because you were my best friend! Now that day and journey have come, and you aren't here to share it. We can't have lunch with each other and do whatever Dads and daughters do. I miss you more than I ever have because I'm off to ONU and you aren't here with me. I love and miss you, Dad. Hope you are having a blast with our Creator!

Sydney and her Dad, Ken

Sonya Johnson Fritz
SISTER

Sonya, Ken's older sister, and Ken

I've been thinking a lot and needed to put some thoughts on paper. There has been a lot of talk about my brother as a friend, mentor, CEO, business partner, business owner, Department Chair, father, son, and husband. Kenny was also a brother, a baby brother 6 years my junior. He was the archetypal annoying little brother. I nicknamed him Kenema, or just "enema" for short. He was hyper as anything, he was a poor loser, a boastful winner, and loved playing Monopoly, which he always won.

As he got older, I was the test for any incoming girlfriend. There was one girl who was scared to death to meet me because Kenny told her I was the one who had the say in whether or not she got the family's blessing. "You'd better impress her," he said.

On the weekends when he came home from ONU, he and some buddies would stop by my house and play endless hours of their newest video games. They devoured a lot of pizza in those days.

As an adult, Ken transformed from a little brother to a "big brother," not just because he was taller than I am, which is not an achievement, but also because of the role he took on in my life. During a difficult time, he provided refuge and a means of retreat, protection, support, and assistance. In the summer of 2008, Kenny and I had a long talk about our relationship and how the family dynamics have affected both of us. That was a first and much-needed conversation and brought about much healing for both of us. We decided to develop a non-verbal cue just between us that would remind us everything was okay when things that had once brought division would surface.

I'm so thankful for the last conversation my brother and I had about 2 months before his passing. The conversation was difficult to approach, but I'm thankful both of us gave each other the time and patience to really hear the other out. The hour and a half we talked brought about resolution and ended with "I love you." Thank you for letting me share just a bit about Kenny, the brother.

Brittany Weideman Cirone
NIECE

Ken and oldest niece, Brittany

Although there are thousands to choose from, one of my favorite memories of Uncle Ken happened at church camp. He always played this game where he would hold up a five dollar bill, and we would open up our hands about a foot underneath his and try to catch the money. If we caught it, we could keep it. The game is a lot more challenging than it sounds. One by one we would keep on trying, and nobody could do it. As time went by, Uncle Ken got cockier after each unsuccessful attempt. After all my cousins had a turn, he decided to exchange the five dollar bill for a crisp twenty. He obviously wanted to up the ante. After waiting in line, it was my turn. I walked up to Uncle Ken and gave him a little smirk and put my hands under his. As he dropped Andrew Jackson, by both our luck, I caught it. The look on his face was priceless, and I will never forget that moment.

I wish I could give him a huge hug and tell him how much I love him. My uncle touched so many people's hearts here, and inspired so many people. He was quite the popular guy. God knows he was special and that he could change people's lives.

Whitnie Johnson McNeil
SISTER

Ken started high school as a Brady Bunch look--alike with his permed hair, and by the time high school was over, he was a blonde, suave macho man. Ken's college years and life after were consumed with becoming a man with a degree in engineering and starting his newly married life with his wife, Jen. I was working for a research company, and Ken needed money for Jen's engagement ring. I needed participants for a normal skin study to sell some skin for money. Ken became one of my first subjects.

Ken was always up for fun as he played games with nieces and nephews, going camping, worldwide traveling, enjoying his children and wife, and giving to those in need.

About three years ago, one bitterly cold winter day after I spent the night at my parents' house, my car wouldn't start, and I needed a new battery. My mother and I went to get a new battery. For my Chrysler, replacing the battery was not a simple task. The right front tire had to be removed, then the battery, housed under the right front fender, in an awkward position, had to be disconnected and removed and the new one installed. Then we had to put it all back together. It took all afternoon for my brother to accomplish the task in the driveway of my mom and dad's house. I am thankful Ken did not get frostbitten and will be forever grateful for the kind and thoughtful brother that he was.

Ken was full of lots of energy and was a very hyper child, always entertaining children and acting like he was falling and doing goofy stunts. Little kids absolutely loved him. He loved making forts out of blankets, chairs, and pillows. In our elementary years, this was almost a daily occurrence, taking up entire rooms in the house. Ken also loved Monopoly. He was a very competitive player and took it seriously. Sometimes these games would last for days and weeks, laid out on the floor or table. One time, he was doing the *Greased Lightning* song on our coffee table, which had a glass top. Near the end of the song, where John Travolta jumped off of the car, Ken jumped off of the coffee table and broke the glass. He loved that song, though.

The last memory I have with Ken was when our whole family was together, and I had a secret game and needed two volunteers. Being up for the adventure, Ken volunteered. He was up against my dad, so his competitiveness totally kicked in. They had a majorly frozen shirt in a ball and had to unfreeze it then put it on. From the microwave to hot water, to pulling and tugging he won proudly, putting the icicle t-shirt on when he was finished. He had a free and loving spirit I will surely miss.

Kristie McNeil
NIECE

How do you celebrate a life, a person, with just words and paper? How do you describe the influence and the importance a person brought to your life with simply sentences and punctuation?

You can't. You don't.

You can, however, remember the memories and celebrate the influences a life had on yours. My Uncle Ken influenced my life in great and multiple ways. Time is such a fragile object—an abstract object—but an object nonetheless. It can be taken from you suddenly, and what at one second seems so unfathomable and unrelenting can be wiped clean and disappear the next. As Christians, we often lose a sense of that urgency of time; we think time will wait for us, and we can share Christ when it's convenient and we're ready. My Uncle Ken didn't let time wait for him, and he didn't wait for time, either.

One of the most influential attributes about Uncle Ken was his deep desire for missions. I saw his drive for spreading God's grace and at the same time bettering the lives of those around the world, in whatever shape and fashion he saw needed. Uncle Ken had an honest heart for serving and sharing the Lord.

In November 2013, I was wrestling with the idea of going on my first international missions trip; I've always felt a pull toward missions, but I wasn't sure if it was the right time for me to spread my wings toward another country. As I was struggling with this situation, I received a devastating and life-altering call from my mother—my young, healthy, seamlessly wonderful Uncle Ken had passed away suddenly and unexpectedly.

How could God allow a man who was so devoutly after Christ's own heart to be taken from this world? It didn't make sense and it didn't seem fair.

But I've come to realize something: Uncle Ken's life was a testimony. A 43-year testimony of the amazing love of Christ and what can be accomplished if you allow Christ to work in you. At my Uncle Ken's funeral, I remember somebody speaking these exact words, "We should all follow after the life Ken lived and carry on his heart for missions and his desire to reach the world for Christ." At that moment, I knew I was to go and be part of an international missions team for the then upcoming summer; I knew I needed to live as Uncle Ken had and go serve Christ throughout the world.

In June of 2014, I went to India for 2 weeks. It was my first time being overseas and my first time experiencing God in another country. My Uncle Ken's influence and drive toward spreading the word of the Lord has played richly into my life, and I am filled with an unquenchable desire to go serve the Lord, a desire that was sparked by the desire to serve the Lord that I saw within my Uncle.

Although this missions trip was something I had prayed about and truly sought God's guidance for, I think my Uncle Ken's testimony and beautiful example of serving God and my desire to carry on missions in a way my Uncle Ken did was a major influencer that inched me on my way to missions. I believe God used Ken Johnson, a dazzling man after God's own heart, a man who I am so blessed to call my uncle, as His way of showing me that missions was a part of God's plan for my life. My Uncle Ken was, and will forever live on as, a man who was after the heart of Christ and wanted everyone to have the knowledge to have that same heart.

Amy McNeil
NIECE

Last year Uncle Ken, Aunt Jen, and my cousins attended my graduation party. They drove 8 hours just to attend the party for my twin sister and me in Alpena, MI. They could only stay for about four hours before they had to drive back to Kankakee. Not everyone is willing to do that. It meant more to me than anything in the world to have them there, and the sacrifice they made driving 16 hours did not go unnoticed. Uncle Ken also taught me to keep the faith, no matter what. His faith was one of the best examples I've had. No matter what life gave him, he always turned to God and knew God was in control. The memories of the games, my graduation, the African food, and his faith are what help me get through rough days because they are memories that make me smile.

Stephanie McNeil
NIECE

There was never a dull moment when Uncle Ken was around. One time, we had a big dinner at our grandparents' house. Grandma made some African curry for dinner that night. Uncle Ken had this gross habit of relating everything we ate to an animal and its body parts. He made our food sound really nasty. Don't get me wrong, I still ate it. Even if his story repulsed me, I knew he was kidding, and I knew the food would still taste good.

Melissa Woudstra Fessenden
NIECE

Ken Johnson. Uncle Ken to me, so many memories and no words to truly and accurately describe them. Ken was a man from whom Godly wisdom seemed to flow so freely, yet somehow you never felt "less" around him. Growing up he always seemed to me to be sandwiched between genera-tions, or maybe a bridge between them would more adequately describe it. He was older than I and in the next stage of life, and I looked to Ken and Jenny as being where I would be in a few short years. Somehow, as a child it was much easier to glimpse adulthood when looking at them. To me, they were what I hoped I would be as an adult.

Ken was the "cool" uncle: someone who invested in his nieces and nephews and made us feel important and included. Ken was the one who taught me to drive a stick shift, in his Porsche no less. I still can't believe he trusted me behind the wheel, and I still remember how much it meant to me that he did. Ken always encouraged imagination and well thought out plans. In our adolescent years, he had us completely convinced there were Indians in the woods surrounding our yearly camping grounds. This was cemented in reality for us when Ken took us for walks in the woods near dark. We listened together to the Indians drumming, uncovered their used campfire sites, and traced their moccasin tracks with our small fingers. Ken brought everything to life with such excitement that one couldn't help but get caught up in the flow of it. He had us write our own movies and act them out as he directed and recorded them in the campground and the surrounding woods and dunes. There were time capsules and dangerous twists and turns. There were wonderful endings and tragic ones, much like life.

As we grew up and married, Ken continued to be a source of wisdom and knowledge for both us and our spouses. He was the one we could freely talk to about anything. He was always interested in our lives and listened well, giving tidbits here and there that stick in my mind to this day. It was Ken who first gave my husband and me biblical financial advice by which we still live and share with others. He told us, "So many say 'I give God the first 10 percent of my money,' but it should be that 100 percent of our money is the Lord's. We give Him back the first 10 percent and the remaining 90 percent we are stewards of. It's all God's."

It's all God's. That was how Ken lived his life.

When I heard Ken got the job at ONU, I remember thinking I couldn't picture a better place for him to be. I thought of all the college students he would come into contact with every day and knew they would be blessed to know him as I had been. I think Ken shaped the course of many lives while he was here, mine being only one of them. I will never understand why Ken had to go home when he did, but I know the Lord will turn it around and use it for His good. Ken was one of the single most influential people I have known, and I am so joyfully thankful to God for every moment spent with him. Ken will be remembered by all who knew him, and the mission he started has only just begun.

Austin Talbott
NEPHEW

There is hardly a day, hour, or minute that goes by I don't think of my Uncle Ken. He was like my second father. I will always remember the trips we took together, the board games we played, and all the basketball games he played with me, my dad, and my brother Nicholas.

Bill Jones
UNCLE

Kenny was my nephew, and though Elaine and I did not see as much of him as we would have liked, we always knew he was a special part of our extended family.

Our impressions of Ken came from our very brief visits, often when Ken was traveling near where we were. He always made an extra effort to call Elaine when she was in DC, or visit Todd in Las Vegas, or stop by Gettysburg with the family when they were headed toward the Jersey Shore.

We already knew, from phone calls with Jerri and Dave, that Kenny's life had a star quality. He excelled in school and immediately got a job where he could climb the corporate ladder to the very top. But he was not content to be the boss or make money; he followed his passions and found a new calling at Olivet, where he could use his talents to help others become all they could be.

I had seen in our brief visits he was an incredibly earnest and engaging young man who wanted to know all he could about everyone he met. He was always positive, humble, and straight forward with a disarming humor. We liked him a lot.

When my sister called and told us he was gone, we couldn't believe it. Like Jerri, we were devastated at the loss of this gifted nephew, knowing the effect his death would have on the whole family. We are so glad we were able to come for his funeral services, and get to know Ken in a whole different way.

In Matthew 7, an often repeated verse jumps out at my wife and me: "By their fruits you shall know them." In the short time we were in Kankakee, we saw what impact Ken had on ONU's campus community and all the faculty and students he knew. There was an enormous outpouring of love for Ken from every person we met. It was clear Ken had made the most of his time on earth. He had so many "soul mates," along with his loving family, and the untold number of people who called him their "best friend."

At the ceremony, he was lauded as a man of faith with a big brain and a bigger heart. He was big into being a dad, big into being a husband, and big into being the beloved son and brother to his sisters. He left a hole in the family that can never be filled, but he left a legacy that will never be ignored or forgotten.

Ken Johnson, precious nephew, by your fruits, nurtured by your big heart, you will forever be known and dearly loved.

Ruth Ann Jones Miller
AUNT

My nephew, Ken Johnson—Kenny to me—was very special to our family. He is my sister's only son, my younger son's best friend, my older son's hunting and soccer buddy, my daughters' only male cousin they grew up with, and one of my husband's loved and respected hunting partners. These connections, however, only serve to describe a piece of our relationships with him. We knew him first because we shared a blood connection; but it grew into much more than that. We liked and respected him.

As a child, when he ran around endlessly and seemingly aimlessly, his activity level was only increased by the pharmaceuticals that were supposed to slow him down. He was very "enthusiastic." However, in due time, his lust for life took on a sense of direction, and his intentionality took on a resolve to "run the race" God was setting before him. There was no stopping the keen curiosity that drove him to welcome new people, new cultures, new ideas, and to satisfy his thirst for new insights and novel discoveries. All these qualities kept the optimism alive that says, "I know we can make it work! I know we can do it!" He always encouraged others to go for it as well. A problem was to be solved; a barrier was to be overcome.

Some of that barrier-busting spirit was lived out in our basement and backyard during visits in the summer when he was a boy. Kenny and my son Ryan both grew up to become engineers, but their inventiveness started in childhood. I vividly recall the day I came home to find the front door to our house propped open and smoke coming out. Alarmed, I ran in to see what was happening. Kenny and Ryan had been "producing" one of their many videos in our basement with our camcorder and their various props. They used dry ice in their "sorcerer's caldron" to create the vapor that was to provide cover, as they used a wand to make a rat, played by our helpless hamster, disappear.

As part of their plot, they had thrown a smoke bomb into our crawl space. My naïve youngest daughter was in that crawl space waiting for her cue to jump out through the smoke. However, my budding directors did not correctly calculate the amount of smoke produced by a smoke bomb thrown into a crawl space, nor did they anticipate the real choking and panic expressed on their young actress' face as she plunged out of the crawlspace in fear. Since the basement door was so close to the front door of our house, both doors had been opened to let the smoke and vapor out of our basement. I wish I could say my daughter's trauma and my reaction to this experiment dulled their enthusiasm for trying something new, but it didn't even come close.

Over the years, Kenny continued to show energy and determination in making the things in which he believed happen. Those which revealed his deepest passion were the ones he believed were given to him by God. He loved getting others involved in these pursuits, and he was good at it. He really believed it was in the best interest of everyone to get involved in something bigger than themselves, even in seemingly small ways.

For Kenny, making something work out often required him to get more people on board. Just 2 weeks before his death, I was visiting my sister in Kankakee where she and her husband were living not far from Ken and his family. She invited them over for dinner so we could visit. Ken was just a year and a half into being the head of the engineering department at ONU. As usual, he was very excited about the opportunities this position provided. I don't think anyone would be able to fully articulate all his creative vision for the future of that department and the students it impacted. I doubt his brain ever stopped dreaming, like the little Kenny who could not stop running when he was small.

After their arrival at my sister's house and as soon as our hellos and hugs were over, Kenny turned to me and said, "Aunt Ruth, can you do me a favor? Now if you can't, just say so, it's okay." Well, I know better than to say "yes" to Kenny without hearing the request. He was a charming manipulator, a fact I write with no animosity. He did not hide his urgency for the answer he wanted, and the request was simple. He had 12 young women from the engineering department set to go to an engineering conference in Baltimore, MD. He believed this conference would help to foster a greater understanding of engineering as a profession with broad opportunities. He also saw it as a significant opportunity for them to connect with other female engineers. One of his goals was to increase the number of females majoring in engineering, and he wanted to get them excited about their career choice. That was important to him.

The simple request, "Since you live about half way between Kankakee and Baltimore, could the twelve college students spend the night at your house? It would save them money and break up the long drive. What do you think?" Then with an encouraging smile on his face he waited for my "yes," which I quickly gave.

I have never regretted Kenny inviting those young women to spend the night at our house. They were absolutely delightful. Many of them, having heard his love for missions, couldn't wait to go on the upcoming mission trip to Swaziland. But, more than that, I could clearly see how his gusto had spilled over on them. They loved him, and they really believed he cared about them, too. One of the ways he was showing his care was to find a way to save them money and make the long drive from Kankakee to Baltimore less taxing. I am so grateful he encouraged me to be a small part of his God-given vision for them

Rob Miller
COUSIN

My experience with Kenny goes back to my childhood. In the early years, I spent most of my time picking on Kenny and my brother Ryan. They were both my little brothers. We grew up together at Thanksgiving, on hunting trips, and during the summers. We would hide in barns and shoot each other with paint guns. As we got older and went to college, I gave Ken advice about his relationship with Jenny, whom he would later marry. At his bachelor party, we made him strip down to his underwear and play the piano. We got a good laugh.

Kenny started a soccer club and brought me in to run an annual camp, which lasted for 8 years. We would play golf and go boating. Later Kenny became Dr. Johnson. One of his greatest qualities was never acting like he was smarter than you, even though he was. He was intelligent and gifted with people. He was Dr. Johnson to some, but will always be Kenny to me. I will always miss the brotherly relationship we had, but I will cherish the awesome experiences. He had a zest for life. He loved his children and was a great Christian example.

Robyn Miller Rogers
COUSIN

My cousin Kenny was just another thorn in my side, along with my brother, and Kenny's best friend, Ryan. Growing up, they both enjoyed the great task of somewhat torturing my younger sister Rebecca (Becca) and me. Kenny would come to our home in Ohio, from his home in Michigan, and the two would get their brilliant minds together to see what they could come up with to do to us. They would sneak in our rooms with markers to try to draw on our faces while we were asleep. I was a very light sleeper and, just when they were about to strike, I would wake up and yell at them. Becca wasn't so lucky, and they got her almost every time. They also put fish food in Becca's mouth and scary things in her bed. They would set traps and tie these little explosive devices to different doors that would explode when you closed or opened them.

Sometimes we would have fun when Kenny and Ryan created their famous home movies. We would all dress up like characters from the *Rocky* movies, and I loved being the girlfriend of Rocky with my mom's fur coat draped around me. I liked Kenny and Ryan during those times. I don't know how Becca felt when she was forced to be characters in their films and got shot at while running across the backyard with literal flaming arrows they shot at her with their bows. Somehow, we survived it all. Kenny and I ended up at ONU together, and it was nice to see a slowly emerging mature person. He met a wonderful girl, Jenny, and seemed quite taken with her. She was a great find for Kenny and proved to be the best wife in the world for him.

The best trait of Kenny's, in my opinion, was his ability to make everyone believe anything was possible. Every challenge that came in the way of your goal, Kenny could put a positive spin on it, and you would believe it was a blessing in disguise. Nothing was too lofty to achieve and you were always capable of doing what you wanted to do. I naturally tend to be a more negative person and get discouraged by obstacles. Kenny never appeared, to me anyway, to get defeated. He was either the greatest con man in the world or he really believed anything could be done. I know it was the latter. With this attitude, he had great vision and great plans.

He saw endless possibilities to serve others at all times and wherever he was at any point in his life. Whether it was helping a small struggling church, a personal friend in need, students on the campus of a college, or the people he loved so much in Kenya and Swaziland, his optimism, his ability to dream, and his genuine love for others couldn't be matched. It was special. Kenny was a man of great purpose and integrity. I am thankful Kenny touched my life, even though we didn't always get along. What was once a thorn, God blessed and became a rose.

Rebecca Miller Anderson
COUSIN

My cousin Ken, or Kenny as I liked to call him, was an intricate part of my childhood and a good friend in adulthood. When I think about my summers and holidays spent with Kenny and his family growing up, I think of forts in the woods, going inner-tubing at their friends' cabin, playing "Ghost in the Graveyard," making home movies, and playing pranks on each other while sleeping. I think about going to amusement parks, playing Rook for hours on end, and watching *St. Elmo's Fire* 50 times. In fact, I think Kenny taught me how to play the theme song on the piano. Kenny, my brother Ryan, Erica, and I were a force to be reckoned with. The boys would gang up on us and hold us hostage in Ken's fort in the woods or sneak in at night to paint our faces while we were sleeping. They thought they were brilliant by setting various booby traps around themselves at night so we couldn't retaliate; but we always managed to maneuver through those traps.

I have so many fond memories of water skiing and swimming out to the dock at Ken's friends' cabin. One particularly vivid memory took place during one summer when I was probably around eleven years old. Ken was maybe 13. It was dusk; the sun was just setting. Kenny and I were each in these really cool rafts like lounge chairs that float. The water and the air were a perfect temperature, almost like a cooling bath. The rafts were chained to the dock, so we were just gently floating in the water. The moon was beginning to rise and the stars were starting to dot the sky. I remember feeling so relaxed, almost euphoric. After a while of just floating in bliss, I looked over at Kenny and he said in this impassioned tone, "I am so comfortable." I just chuckled and said, "Me too."

In adulthood, Ken and I remained good friends. We even continued making summer memories with camping trips and trips to the state fair and amusement parks through our college years. Following marriage and babies, it was challenging to keep up regular visits with Jen and the kids; however, I am grateful to have had an annual visit with Ken during hunting season. Ken was actually very helpful to me several times while I was working to improve our financial situation and reduce debt through Dave Ramsey's principals. I called Ken several times to receive advice in this area since he had been so successful with the program and became a leader in it. Ken was always genuinely excited about helping and blessing others with his resources.

I am very grateful to have had an extended visit with Kenny not long before he passed away. We spent the night with him and his family on our way to visit Milwaukee, where we were relocating. When we arrived at Ken's house, he was at urgent care getting a moth removed from his ear canal. It had flown into his ear while he was working in the garage before we arrived. We all had a good laugh when he returned to relay the events of the night to us. We stayed up late that night, and he introduced us to one of his favorite snacks: pretzels dipped in vanilla ice cream. He was shocked we had never tried this delicacy ourselves. We spent hours talking the next day about all life's big questions, family issues, and just stuff about our kids and our lives. We had a great visit, and I am very thankful for that time with him. My memories of time spent with Kenny were always positive, full of joy, energy, laughter, and meaning. I look forward to making new ones in the age to come.

Marie Johnson
COUSIN

Dr. Kenneth Johnson, the beloved son of my first cousin David and his wife Jerri, was born after a long list of Johnson girls whose names would change with marriage. Finally, a boy to carry on the Johnson name! The family jokingly observed that, after waiting so long for a boy, Ken was, had we been royalty, very close to being our Crown Prince! What I remember most about his relationship with the Pennsylvania relatives was how happy he was to see us when we got together every year or so. But then, Ken was happy to see anyone. From the time he was quite small, he had the ability to engage people in conversation, no matter their age or how long they had been acquainted. He seemed to look upon everyone as a friend he had not yet met.

Ken had a "joie de vivre" that was contagious. He hardly sat still and was always organizing a game of some kind. Being so athletic, he was constantly tossing a ball of some kind, convincing others to get away from the food table and get some exercise. And oh, what fun we had! Although Ken was an exceptional athlete, he took time to encourage the younger Johnsons, the older Johnsons, and any other Johnsons who weren't as adept at the game. He would patiently help youngsters hold a bat or toss a pitch for the first time, often holding up the game while the rest of us roasted in the sun. Ken was a born teacher, whether it was tutoring his own children, instructing his college classes in engineering, or delivering the good news of Jesus' love to tribes in Kenya. He was happiest when he was helping others.

Ken loved to hear stories about the three Johnson brothers, his grandfather included, and the Swedish heritage that came to our country with our forefathers, Anna and Olaf. He was thrilled to travel from Michigan to New York City to find their names on the Wall of Immigrants at Ellis Island. What a great trip that was—a whole caravan heading to the Big Apple to celebrate our heritage!

When our Swedish cousin Sven came to America for a visit with his family, Ken again made the trip to Pennsylvania to meet them and ask questions about his great grandfather's side of the family. When some of them returned a few years later, Ken was happy to entertain them in his beautiful home in Michigan and show them a bit more of the country.

Much has been said about Ken's love and compassion for everyone he met. That is certainly undisputed. We can't begin to speculate why he was taken so early from all who loved him. We can only gain comfort from knowing he is hidden away in God's heart. And so it is fitting for the English teacher I am to finish my tribute with the much-used quote from *Hamlet*, "Good night, sweet Prince. And flights of angels sing thee to thy rest." Much love to you, Ken. We miss you.

Appendix B
Reflections from Students and Others

Dr. Shane Ritter
CHAIR, DEPARTMENT OF ENGINEERING

I never met Dr. Ken Johnson, not in person, anyway. But he has affected my life and the life of my family tremendously. You see, I am the person who took Ken's place as the chair of the engineering department at ONU. The crazy thing is, for all practical purposes, Ken is the very person who hired me. Let me explain, and in the process give my story about Ken Johnson.

I have been working in the electrical engineering field for the last 25 years, and during that time, I have acquired my BS, MS, and PhD in electrical engineering. I have been a Christian for longer, and for the last 25 years have always struggled with balancing my professional life and my spiritual life. While I have experienced measured success in engineering, I always felt something was missing, and I was convinced there must be some way to combine my two worlds of faith and work. For years, I struggled with this, even exploring the possibility of going to seminary and leaving engineering for a life of full-time ministry.

Every time I would do this, I always gently sensed the Lord telling me I was already called to the full-time ministry. This being the case, I continued to struggle to balance or combine my two worlds. I eventually began working in foreign missions, and by God's grace, I was led to I-TEC, which is an electrical engineering missions organization. While this did provide some fulfillment, I still sensed there was more. I continued to wrestle with this year after year. In the more intense times of my struggle, I would sometimes do random Internet searches for "Christian electrical engineers" and things like that just to see what was out there. It was during one of these times that I got a hit on my search. It was for a full-time electrical engineering professor at ONU.

While I had some discussions and interest from other Christian colleges before, they either never seemed all that genuine or they required my family and me to relocate at a time when that was simply not possible. Reluctantly, I sent in my application materials and told God he would have to work a miracle for this to pan out. About a week later, I received an email from Ken, asking me if I had time to talk with him on the phone. We chose a time, and I reluctantly agreed to speak with him; all the while my wife expressed she had no desire to relocate to Bourbonnais, IL from our location in Charlotte, NC.

The time for the call came, and Ken and I spoke for about 2 hours. It is hard to describe, but I know many other Christians, and I have expressed the feeling when meeting another Christian brother who, even though we just met, it felt like we had known each other for a long time. In my mind, this is more of a spiritual connection. I expressed much of what I had been experiencing in my professional and spiritual life, and Ken shared with me he had been experiencing the exact same thing. We shared our thoughts and experiences, and it was uncanny how similar they were and how we had both been struggling with some of the same things. It was evident to my wife after this conversation this was much more than another phone interview; this was potentially a providential appointment.

Ken and I spoke one more time on the phone when he called and asked if I would come to ONU for an on-campus interview. We did not speak for long this time, but the connection was still there. I agreed to come, but there was an obstacle to overcome. Ken said they already had a candidate scheduled to come for an interview in about 3 weeks and that I would need to wait until after that interview was done before I could schedule my interview. This seemed like a long wait, but I agreed. This would be the last time that I would ever speak with Ken. We had a couple of email exchanges after, but that is all. After about 2 weeks of waiting, I quite randomly went to the website of ONU when I noticed on the home page an announcement that they were mourning the loss of the chair of the engineering department next to a picture of Ken. It really did not sink in at first exactly what they were saying, so I had to read the announcement several times. I could hardly believe what I was reading.

I was devastated by the news and confused as to what this meant for the process of my interview.

While I eventually got the position, it was difficult to lose the connection I had briefly formed with Ken. The more time I spend at ONU, the more I see just how impactful Ken was. This program owes so much to his work and vision; without Ken's passions for engineering, teaching, and missions, ONU would not have the successful program it does.

Rachel Groters
OFFICE MANGER DEPARTMENT OF ENGINEERING, ADJUNCT PROFESSOR, DEPARTMENT OF ENGLISH AND MODERN LANGUAGES

As a senior at ONU, I worked part-time in the Engineering department as a clerical assistant. My senior year was also Ken's first year as Engineering's Chair. I didn't work with him closely then, but I could tell that he was focused on action and progress. I had no idea how much he was focused on these things until I began working with him closely the following year, when I came back to work for Engineering as the Office Manager. Ken was a blast to work with, and he kept me on my toes! There was always a new project to work on that I'd be drafted into at the last second. But pulling it off was an adventure and added spice and variety to my job—I legitimately loved it. Whenever I think of Ken, two things come to mind: first, whether or not he actually espoused this himself, I think his mantra was "Ask for forgiveness rather than permission." He wouldn't take no for an answer and always found a way to get 'er done. As someone who is prone to stop trying the first time I'm told something's not possible, I really admired this about Ken. Second, when I think of how Ken did things metaphorically, I imagine him driving along in a big bandwagon, beckoning to people and telling them to jump aboard. Ken was always plowing ahead, but he didn't leave people behind in his wake. He invited people to take his journeys with him. And his inviting spirit made each person he interacted with, including me, feel very special and capable. I wish that I had known more about Ken when he was still alive. He was so action-oriented, and I was so busy helping him in his endeavors, that I didn't take the time to understand his heart. But I found out after he passed away what a great man he really was and how big his heart was for the Lord and for people, especially his students. Working with him was a true privilege and has left an indelible impact on my life and leadership.

Wes Gerbig
COORDINATOR, MASTER OF ENGINEERING MANAGEMENT PROGRAM

Ken Johnson was an unknown to me when he hired on to ONU as the Engineering Program Chair. I wondered who this man was and what he would do with a program that was very near and dear to my heart. Almost before I could complete that thought, Ken had reached out to me to see if I had some opportunities to advance the program; could I place students in internships or host a senior project? Coincidentally I had recently made a connection to a Nazarene Missionary who was using micro industry to improve the lives of the people of Thailand; he was doing this by building and selling high end bamboo bicycles. Ken jumped on this chance to bring a missional project on board for the program and asked me to serve as a day to day mentor to the students in lieu of a company representative, as they were literally half way around the world. When Ken made such a request, it was hard to say no. Not because he pressured you but because he compelled you through his passion and energy. He made you feel unique in your ability to perform the task at hand and perhaps that you would be missing out on something big if you didn't make this investment of time. This feeling was, in fact, very accurate based on his track record.

Throughout the experience of visiting campus to mentor this group of students, Ken and I formed a friendship that felt like it extended far beyond its short duration. Ken shared that he had conversations planned with the graduate school to launch a Masters in an Engineering related discipline. Again, with an offer that included the fear of missing out on something big, Ken encouraged me to partner with him in constructing a graduate program to partner with the undergraduate engineering program. Again, I just couldn't say no. Ken and I collaborated on that vision over the next few months and prepared a presentation for the administration of the University to formally propose the Master of Engineering Management. Sadly, Ken's passing came less than two weeks prior to the presentation. The administration and I decided it best to not let up with the progress and instead to push this program forward in Ken's honor. So that's what we did, and what we continue to do.

Ken managed to deliver a lifetime of impact into less than 2 years at ONU, I can only imagine the impact that he delivered throughout other stages of his life. I am a better man for having known him, understand better how to honor God through vocation, and miss Ken every time he crosses my mind.

Parker Shelton
CLASS OF 2016

One thing that I will always remember was that Dr. Johnson helped me prepare for my internship. I had no idea what to expect, and he was able to inform me of what I might be doing according to my job title.

Neil Smith
CLASS OF 2015

When Dr. Johnson came to ONU, he got right to work and started a design for the new engineering building and got the accreditation for computer engineering through. I think Dr. Johnson's hard work, persistence, and Christian attitude toward people and life was a real example for other students and me.

Kaleb Sollar
CLASS OF 2014

Dr. Johnson was always filled with so much wisdom. Every class he had so much to say about the workplace outside ONU. He knew so much, and he knew how to communicate with us. He was able to pick up on whether we were understanding the material or not. He provided great examples and real applications, and he always seemed to know the best way to explain something to us. He truly loved his students, and we all felt that.

Preston Shelton
CLASS OF 2016

My most impressionable image was during a pick-up game of basket-ball. Dr. Johnson drove up the lane and finished a layup over me. He was showing he could still cut it even if he was an "old man".

Taylor Schott
CLASS OF 2016

The first time I met Dr. Johnson was on the basketball court in Birchard Gymnasium. I recognized him as our Department Chair, but I did not know him beyond that. On the court, he was a friend. He was no longer a teacher, mentor, or leader, but he was our friend who played basketball with us. Ken could play basketball, too; although he was not as fast as he might once have been, he could pass the ball like Steve Nash and set others up on the court to score points.

Beyond basketball, Dr. Johnson had a huge impact on my goals. I want to be involved with Engineering Missions International. When I gradu-ate, I want to use my skills to benefit others with what I have learned; Dr. Johnson inspired that earnest desire. He took what he knew from the business world, also the Christian aspect, and brought it to us at ONU. He has been one of the biggest influences I've had, and he directly contrib-uted to my sense of purpose in using my engineering degree to further the Kingdom.

Aaron Lucas
CLASS 2013

I will never forget the times I got to interact with Dr. Johnson. I remem-ber when he first came to ONU to give a presentation to all the students so we could see if we liked him. After that, I knew that he would be an awesome person to take over the position of Engineering Department Chair. After my senior year started, I was disappointed I would only be able to have him as a professor for one Senior Design class. He was such a great professor. I learned so much from him in just that one class. I enjoyed just sitting in the lab while he was teaching other classes so I could listen in and learn more from courses I had already taken.

I remember having a conversation with Ken about Missioneering. We were sitting around talking about missions and engineering and trying to figure out a word or group of words that we could use to describe it. Missioneering came to mind, and after I said it, Ken ran with it. I never fully understood how much he liked that term until I found out he was using it every day while teaching classes and having it put on shirts to give out to people. I will never forget having this one conversation with him.

Garrett Muhlstadt
CLASS 2016

Dr. Johnson moved into my neighborhood the summer before I started at ONU, and my brother and his son became good friends. I would often play wiffleball with his kids in their yard, and I would get to talk to him sometimes. He certainly loved his family, and I loved how he would talk up each of his children based on their different strengths. Over the summer, he talked to me about engineering and at one point asked me if I was reviewing my calculus. Normally, I wouldn't have, but since he asked about it, I certainly did.

He also had a vision about things as simple as his yard at his house. At one point, he was talking to me about it, pointing to the spots in the yard where he would put in a volleyball net and a soccer field. He always seemed to have the bigger picture in mind. He was truly a great example for treating every day like your last.

Muaz Faroog
CLASS 2016

Whenever I wanted help on something or to discuss anything, Dr. Johnson never said, "No". I remember the first time when I went to his office and asked if he had time to talk to me his words were, "I am here for you guys, come in!" He knew how to show how much he cared about others.

Daniel Going
CLASS 2015

I had just talked to a friend the day Dr. Johnson passed away about how I was going to go into his office on Monday to talk to him about my future, about internships, and how to handle those new experiences. And then I got word an hour later and was just absolutely heartbroken it would never happen; his wealth of experience and knowledge was gone, just like that. I felt so lost during those first few months because the one person in my field to whom I genuinely looked up to was no longer and could no longer be in my life. I want to keep the memories I have of him as someone who woke up every day with a hardcore passion for learning and engineering.

Ryan Kee
CLASS 2014

Dr. Johnson was committed to teaching so students could pass the Fundamentals of Engineering exam, but he was more determined to make sure they were prepared for the real world and real life problems. Dr. Johnson was open, honest, hardworking, respectable, funny, kind, and intelligent. He not only cared about our academic minds, but he also cared about our spiritual lives as well.

Taylor Westrate
CLASS 2014

Before Dr. Johnson's passing, I'd never really experienced death, especially nothing that sudden. I guess a positive that can be taken from what happened is that my ideas on how to best live life changed. I realized how short life really can be, so making every day count is a decent philosophy to have, regardless of its cliché. Dr. Johnson was exactly what the Engineering Department needed and he can't be replaced. A man of his character and diverse knowledge does not come around every day, and he is a man whose influence in my life I will miss sorely.

Zane DeBeck
CLASS 2016

Dr. Johnson was a very take-charge person, and he wasn't able to let limitations get in his way; that is really how we should all live. Dr. Johnson was very genuine, and he always gave God the glory of everything that he did; everything about him was centered in God. I loved that he was always up to a new challenge, and he did so very successfully. I have always wanted to be a leader and impact lives, and he had both of those very strong qualities. He had so much to offer during the mission trip and even around the engineering department. He was always willing to devote his time to others. I have always wanted to be a professor as well; I just did not realize when I wanted to be one. I believe he inspired me to enter into the professorial world sooner than I had originally chosen.

Taylor Williams
CLASS OF 2016

Dr. Johnson saw in us what we couldn't see ourselves. He knew how much potential we had and that we could fulfill it. He had a tender way of teaching truth. We knew our tasks and lessons were things he had done a thousand times and could easily do, but he took the time to make sure we knew how to do it, too, and that we could do it well. He never missed a teachable moment, and often times, he disguised it as fun or incredibly interesting.

Dr. Mark Quanstrom
PASTOR, COLLEGE CHURCH OF THE NAZARENE, DEAN OF SCHOOL OF THEOLOGY

I didn't know Ken long which means I didn't know him long enough. The first time I met Ken, Jen, and their family was when they came to Sunday school at College Church.

I always like to get to know the people who attend the church I pastor, so I met Ken for breakfast one morning at Blues Café. He started the conversation by saying, "Don't tell me anything about the church. Let me tell you what is going on." He began to describe the internal church dynamics of College Church, and he was exactly right. We probably spent close to 3 hours together in that first breakfast meeting talking about church, work, and family. We walked out to his car, and I had never seen a Nissan leaf (electric). So we took a drive in it while he explained it to me. He then pulled over and he let me drive it. Fun. Following that first breakfast, I knew I had found a new friend. I'm thinking that a lot of people felt that way around Ken, but from that moment on, I eagerly anticipated a lifelong friendship with Ken and his family.

We would see each other at church and at faculty meetings, of course, but we would also intentionally meet for coffee to talk church, work, and family. The last time we met was in the Red Room at ONU, and as always, we were together for several hours. In that short amount of time, I knew that Ken was a man of great integrity and character. He loved his Lord and lived his life purposefully for the sake of His Lord. He had a great sense of humor and our conversation was punctuated by a lot of laughter. I knew that he loved Jen and their four children and that he couldn't have been prouder of them than he was.

But I believe I have come to know Ken more since he has passed away than before. You see, I knew him for less than a year, and we became, in Jen's words, fast friends, but I have known Jen, Sydney, Erick, Luke and Bethany now for almost three years. As their pastor, it has been both Debi's and my privilege to talk with his family through that terrible time of sorrow and then be with them on many occasions since then. I have witnessed his independence, determinations, curiosity, and intelligence in his four wonderful children. I know even more now than I did before he passed away what kind of man he was because his legacy lives on in Jen and his four children.

That makes me miss him more, of course. I'm sad that I didn't get to know him better when he was with his family, but I know more of what kind of man he was because of them.

I have to say that I am really looking forward to the time when we will catch up with each other in the coming Kingdom and we get to spend much more time than 3 hours talking with and truly enjoying each other's company.

Appendix C
Eulogy Virtues

Funeral Service
DR. KEN JOHNSON

Presidential Remarks
JOHN C. BOWLING

College Church of the Nazarene

November 8, 2013

Have you noticed that time seems to stand still for a moment when we first learn that someone we know and love has died? Nothing else matters in that instant. Such moments are shocking and yet helpful in a way, for they force us to push the pause button and hit the mute switch, at least momentarily, so that we might focus singularly on the life of the person who has passed away.

When I got the call last Saturday afternoon that Ken Johnson had died, everything else seemed to stop. My mind immediately shifted from what I was doing to him. His face came to mind; I could see his smile. Then, after a brief moment, that single image gave way to a series of images of him across the last several months.

I first got to know Ken when he came for a faculty interview. There were three things about that moment that impressed me. First, Jen was with him. Her presence told me how much Ken valued her and his family.

Second, he asked how serious we were about building the engineering program. Third, he told how some he had talked to about coming to ONU have said, "Ken you are at the peak of your career, these are your best years—why would you make such a move now?" To which he commented, "Why would I not want to give my best years to this work?"

His time at ONU had only begun, but what he accomplished in that short period of time will last for generations.

We are here to mark his passing, but there is more. His untimely death is the occasion for this service, but not the reason we are here. The reason we are here is that Ken Johnson lived and it is his life (not just his death) that touched each of us.

Although I am a university president, I never speak to a wiser crowd than at a funeral, for in these moments we are forced to look at life through the lens of eternity. And it is that view point which brings life's true values into focus.

David Brooks, the esteemed *New York Times* columnist and commentator, recently reflected on living one's life for your eulogy rather than your resume. He says:

"I've been thinking about the difference between the résumé virtues and the eulogy virtues. The résumé virtues are the ones you put on your résumé, which are the skills you bring to the marketplace. The eulogy virtues are the ones that get mentioned in the eulogy, which are deeper: who are you, are you bold, loving, dependable, and consistent?"

Most of us would say that the eulogy virtues are the more important of the virtues. But at least in my case, are they the ones that I think about the most? The answer is no.

So I've been thinking about that problem, and an individual who has helped me think about it is a guy named Joseph Soloveitchik, who was a rabbi who wrote a book called The Lonely Man of Faith.

He said there are two sides of our natures, which he called Adam I and Adam II. "Adam I is the ambitious, external side of our nature. He wants to build, create, create companies, and create innovation. Adam II is the humble side of our nature. Adam II wants not only to do good, but to be good, to live in a way internally that honors God and our possibilities.

Adam I wants to conquer the world. Adam II wants to hear a calling and obey. Adam I savors accomplishment. Adam II savors inner consistency and strength. Adam I asks how things work. Adam II asks why we're here."

Dr. Ken Johnson had an impressive resume: he could compete with any *Adam I* out there, and he did; but that was not what he lived for. His life was shaped not by the values and priorities of the marketplace; his life was shaped, from an early age, by his faith in Jesus Christ. *And that changes our understanding of his passing.*

As Christians, we are living on the bright side of Easter. We live in light of the resurrection. During the days following Ken's untimely death, I was drawn to the words of Jesus, recorded in John chapter 11. The Lord had been called to the home of his friend Lazarus, who had died unexpectedly. Upon his arrival, Jesus was greeted by a grieving sister, Martha.

In the course of their conversation, Jesus said to her, 'I am the resurrection and the life. The one who believes in me will live, even though they die; and whoever lives by believing in me will never die." Then Jesus asked her the question: "Do you believe this?"

"Yes, Lord," she replied. Her reply must be our reply: we, too, believe in the resurrection and eternal life. Even now, our sense of loss and grief is very real; yet as we hold on to our faith, our faith holds us steady. The Psalmist got it right saying, "Yea, though I walk through the valley of the shadow of death, I will fear no evil; for You are with me; Your rod and Your staff, they comfort me."

Dave and Jerri
FATHER AND MOTHER

We want to add here some of the awards and recognition our son received after his passing. Some of them may seem small, but we want to mention the honors, if only to thank those who gave them. Ken left behind a legacy of love and service, and we hope you can take some piece away and live your life to impact others for Christ as our son did.

- ONU named its Engineering Technology Center in honor of Ken.

- Chief John Kimorgo and the people of Ewaso Ng'iro planted a tree in remembrance of Ken.

- ONU's Football team wore Dr. KJ stickers on their helmets at the Homecoming game which was also the day of Ken's funeral.

- A bench was dedicated to Ken and placed on the Iceman Cometh Trail, near Traverse City, MI.

- The Brighton Church of the Nazarene in Brighton, MI established a missions fund in Ken's honor and name.

- Ken was the subject of a faculty tribute in ONU's yearbook, *Aurora*, the year following his passing.

- Engineering students participated in ONU's Homecoming Tiger Tracks 5K in Ken's memory.

- ONU's annual Servant Leadership Award was given in honor of Ken in 2014.

- A memorial bike ride has been held in Brighton, MI each Memorial Day weekend since his passing.

-Dave and Jerri Johnson

Family picture: Back row : Ken's oldest sister, Sonya, next oldest, Whitnie. Front Row: Dave, Jerri, Erica, Ken's youngest sister, Ken, and our dog Nicki.

Ken, wife Jen, son Luke, daughter Bethany, son Erick, and daughter Sydney; Picture Taken 4 weeks before his passing

Ken playing with kids at a family reunion in our pool in MI

Ryan and Ken

Ken playing soccer for ONU when he was a student

Ken playing the piano

Ken and Jen before they got married

Ken standing on our diving board in MI in the snow.
Trying to show Jen up by going out to our pool and looking like he was going to
dive in. Love and miss you Jen. Eat your heart out Jen. (Jen was in Florida).

Ken's family acting goofy in front of the Statue of Liberty

Ken receiving his PhD at Loughborough University

Ken and his kids having fun

Bethany Johnson, Ken's youngest daughter, drew this
for her mothers birthday last year. Age 13.

Ken's youngest daughter, Bethany Johnson.

Ken

Ken drew this for his mom for a birthday gift when he was 13 years old.
This drawing was made from a picture that our family took in Africa.

About the Authors

Dr. David Johnson was born in Ridgway, PA (a small town in the Allegheny Mts.). After high school, he attended ENC in Quincy, MA, where he met his wife Jerri Jones. Dave taught High School for 3 years, then went to the University of Georgia where he received his Masters' and Doctorate Degrees in Mathematics Education. After graduation, Dave taught at the university level. Dave has held several offices, including Milan Board of Education member for 16 years. As a member of the Michigan Council of Teachers of Mathematics, he served as treasurer, Guidelines Committee member, and Chairman of the Local Arrangements Committee for the Annual M.C.T.M. Conference of 1989. He has also been an invited speaker at numerous Local, State, Regional, National and International Mathematics Education Conferences. Dr. Johnson was Mathematics Advisor for a USAID Curriculum Writing Project for 2 years in Swaziland, Africa. Currently Dave is an Adjunct Professor in the Mathematics Department at ONU.

Jerri was raised in suburban Washington, DC. After high school, she also attended Eastern Nazarene College in Quincy, MA. She and David have been married for 53 years. They have 4 children, 11 grandchildren, and 1 great-grandchild . She was a stay- at- home mom for many years. Jerri created, owned, and managed Weddings with Care, was Vice President of an employment agency, and an interior designer. She is retired and loves being with her children and grandchildren. In her spare time she enjoys interior design, and volunteering at the College Church of the Nazarene University Ave. Bourbonnais IL

CPSIA information can be obtained
at www.ICGtesting.com
Printed in the USA
LVOW11s0122041116

511613LV00001B/10/P